Alternatively, for quick access: simply scan the QR code below to go directly to the product page and request the online resources by filling in the required details.

Happy learning!

Exclusive Online Resources For You

As our valued reader, your purchase of this book includes access to exclusive online resources designed to enhance your learning experience. These resources can be downloaded from our website, www.vibrantpublishers.com, and are designed to help you apply the book's concepts and strategies in practical, measurable ways.

Online resources for this book include the following:

1. **AI Tools Cheat Sheet for Managers:** A quick-reference guide comparing popular AI tools for writing, meetings, productivity, analytics, translation, and customer support, including pricing and key features.
2. **Manager Prompt Library:** A collection of ready-to-use AI prompts for common management tasks such as status reports, difficult conversations, meeting agendas, email responses, brainstorming, performance reviews, and data analysis.
3. **AI Task Suitability Checklist:** A practical framework to help managers determine when AI is appropriate, when human judgment is essential, and when a hybrid approach works best.
4. **AI Pilot Program Communication Templates:** Customizable email templates, meeting scripts, and one-on-one conversation guides for introducing AI initiatives and addressing team concerns.
5. **Responsible AI Use Policy Template:** A structured policy template covering AI governance, approved tools, data handling, transparency, privacy, bias mitigation, and employee responsibilities.

6. **AI Learning and Development Resource Guide:** A curated list of newsletters, podcasts, videos, courses, communities, and tool directories to help managers stay current with AI developments.

Why these online resources are valuable:

- **Immediate implementation:** Provides practical tools and templates that can be used immediately without extensive customization.
- **Manager-focused guidance:** Designed specifically for leadership, communication, decision-making, and team management challenges.
- **Time-saving productivity:** Reduces the effort required to create policies, communications, prompts, and workflows from scratch.

How to access your online resources:

1. **Visit the website:** Go to www.vibrantpublishers.com
2. **Find your book:** Navigate to the book's product page via the "Shop" menu or by searching for the book title in the search bar.
3. **Request the resources:** Scroll down to the "Request Sample Book/Online Resource" section.
4. **Enter your details:** Enter your preferred email ID and select "Online Resource" as the resource type. Lastly, select "user type" and submit the request.
5. **Check your inbox:** The resources will be delivered directly to your email.

SELF-LEARNING MANAGEMENT SERIES

VIBRANT PUBLISHERS

AI ESSENTIALS FOR MANAGERS

Practical ways to boost productivity, make better decisions, and lead high-performing teams

MICHAEL KIENTZ

AI ESSENTIALS FOR MANAGERS

First Edition

Published by Vibrant Publishers LLC, USA, www.vibrantpublishers.com

Paperback ISBN 13: 978-1-63651-747-6
Ebook ISBN 13: 978-1-63651-746-9

Vibrant Publishers' books are available at special quantity discounts for sales promotions, or for use in corporate training programs. For more information, please write to bulkorders@vibrantpublishers.com

Please email feedback/corrections (technical, grammatical, or spelling) to spellerrors@vibrantpublishers.com

Vibrant publishes in a variety of print and electronic formats and by print-on-demand. Some material included with standard print versions of this book may not be included in e-books in print-on-demand. To access the complete catalog of Vibrant Publishers, visit www.vibrantpublishers.com

SELF-LEARNING MANAGEMENT SERIES

TITLE	PAPERBACK* ISBN
BUSINESS AND ENTREPRENEURSHIP	
BUSINESS COMMUNICATION ESSENTIALS	9781636511634
BUSINESS ETHICS ESSENTIALS	9781636513324
BUSINESS LAW ESSENTIALS	9781636511702
BUSINESS PLAN ESSENTIALS	9781636511214
BUSINESS STRATEGY ESSENTIALS	9781949395778
ENTREPRENEURSHIP ESSENTIALS	9781636511603
INTERNATIONAL BUSINESS ESSENTIALS	9781636513294
PRINCIPLES OF MANAGEMENT ESSENTIALS	9781636511542
PRINCIPLES OF MANAGEMENT ESSENTIALS (Sp.Ed)	9781636514994
THE PROFITABLE GOOD	9781636516660
COMPUTER SCIENCE AND TECHNOLOGY	
ARTIFICIAL INTELLIGENCE ESSENTIALS	9781636516387
BLOCKCHAIN ESSENTIALS	9781636513003
CYBERSECURITY ESSENTIALS	9781636514888
DATA STRUCTURES AND ALGORITHMS ESSENTIALS	9781636516325
JAVA ESSENTIALS VOLUME 1	9781636515021
JAVA ESSENTIALS VOLUME 2	9781636516561
MACHINE LEARNING ESSENTIALS	9781636513775
PYTHON ESSENTIALS	9781636512938
DATA SCIENCE FOR BUSINESS	
BUSINESS ANALYTICS ESSENTIALS	9781636514154
BUSINESS INTELLIGENCE ESSENTIALS	9781636513362
BUSINESS STATISTICS ESSENTIALS	9781636514826
DATA ANALYTICS ESSENTIALS	9781636511184
MICROSOFT POWER BI ESSENTIALS	9781636515717

*Also available in Hardback & Ebook formats

SELF-LEARNING MANAGEMENT SERIES

TITLE	PAPERBACK* ISBN
FINANCIAL LITERACY AND ECONOMICS	
COST ACCOUNTING & MANAGEMENT ESSENTIALS	9781636511030
FINANCIAL ACCOUNTING ESSENTIALS	9781636510972
FINANCIAL MANAGEMENT ESSENTIALS	9781636511009
MACROECONOMICS ESSENTIALS	9781636511818
MICROECONOMICS ESSENTIALS	9781636511153
PERSONAL FINANCE ESSENTIALS	9781636511849
PRINCIPLES OF ECONOMICS ESSENTIALS	9781636512334
HR, DIVERSITY, AND ORGANIZATIONAL SUCCESS	
DIVERSITY, EQUITY, AND INCLUSION ESSENTIALS	9781636512976
DIVERSITY IN THE WORKPLACE ESSENTIALS	9781636511122
HR ANALYTICS ESSENTIALS	9781636510347
HUMAN RESOURCE MANAGEMENT ESSENTIALS	9781949395839
LABOR RELATIONS ESSENTIALS	9781636516493
ORGANIZATIONAL BEHAVIOR ESSENTIALS	9781636512303
ORGANIZATIONAL DEVELOPMENT ESSENTIALS	9781636511481
LEADERSHIP AND PERSONAL DEVELOPMENT	
BETTER: A GUIDEBOOK TO A NEW AND IMPROVED YOU	9781636516745
DECISION MAKING ESSENTIALS	9781636510026
INCLUSIVE LEADERSHIP ESSENTIALS	9781636514765
INDIA'S ROAD TO TRANSFORMATION: WHY LEADERSHIP MATTERS	9781636512273
LEADERSHIP ESSENTIALS	9781636510316
PUBLIC SPEAKING ESSENTIALS	9781636516356
TIME MANAGEMENT ESSENTIALS	9781636511665

*Also available in Hardback & Ebook formats

SELF-LEARNING MANAGEMENT SERIES

TITLE	PAPERBACK* ISBN
MODERN MARKETING AND SALES	
BRAND MANAGEMENT ESSENTIALS	9781636515595
CONSUMER BEHAVIOR ESSENTIALS	9781636513263
DIGITAL CONSUMER BEHAVIOR ESSENTIALS	9781636516622
DIGITAL MARKETING ESSENTIALS	9781949395747
MARKETING MANAGEMENT ESSENTIALS	9781636511788
MARKET RESEARCH ESSENTIALS	9781636513744
MODERN ADVERTISING ESSENTIALS	9781636514857
SALES MANAGEMENT ESSENTIALS	9781636510743
SERVICES MARKETING ESSENTIALS	9781636511733
SOCIAL MEDIA MARKETING ESSENTIALS	9781636512181
OPERATIONS MANAGEMENT	
AGILE ESSENTIALS	9781636516417
CONTINUOUS IMPROVEMENT ESSENTIALS	9781636516714
OPERATIONS & SUPPLY CHAIN MANAGEMENT ESSENTIALS	9781949395242
OPERATIONAL EXCELLENCE ESSENTIALS	9781636516592
PRODUCT MANAGEMENT ESSENTIALS	9781636514796
PROJECT MANAGEMENT ESSENTIALS	9781636510712
STAKEHOLDER ENGAGEMENT ESSENTIALS	9781636511511

*Also available in Hardback & Ebook formats

About the Author

Michael Kientz is a leadership development specialist with over 30 years in the field. He has held Director roles with Citi (Citigroup Inc., with a market capitalization of $200 billion) and Compassion International (a non-profit with total revenues of $1.4 billion) and is currently the Director of Training with Crossroads Kids Club, a growing international non-profit. He has led leadership development functions in both the for-profit and non-profit sectors and managed a call center with over 170 staff members. Through his consulting business, *In-Reach Leadership* (established in 2004), he has developed leaders in the government, education, and civic sectors. He has facilitated leadership and team-building workshops across five continents (Africa, Asia, Europe, North America, and South America) and in 24 countries. He has designed several comprehensive leadership development curricula to address the needs of the organizations he has served.

Michael uses AI extensively in his leadership roles as well as in his consulting and writing work. While keeping pace with the rapidly evolving capabilities of AI can be challenging, he enjoys exploring new use cases as they emerge and considers AI an indispensable tool for today's overworked and under-resourced leaders.

Michael is certified in Organization Design, Strategic Workforce Planning, Systems Thinking, Conflict Resolution, Human-Centered Design, and the Myers-Briggs Type

Indicator (MBTI) assessment. He is the author of six previous books and regularly publishes blogs and both short and long videos on YouTube, TikTok, and Instagram. Michael also provides ghostwriting, developmental editing, and coaching services for other authors.

He lived and worked in Thailand for over eight years, supporting leaders and teams throughout Asia. Michael currently lives in Colorado, USA, with his wife of 34 years.

Table of Contents

Part 4: Building Your AI-Ready Plan

Preface

Not long ago, being a capable manager meant mastering the rhythms of people, process, and performance. You learned how to run meetings, make decisions with imperfect information, develop your team, and deliver results. Those fundamentals haven't changed. What has changed is the environment in which you do that work. Artificial intelligence has entered everyday management—not as a distant concept, but as a practical tool shaping decisions, information flow, and how work gets done.

This book is for managers who feel that shift but aren't sure what to do with it. Maybe you're curious, skeptical, or have tried a few tools that felt underwhelming. Or maybe you've seen enough to know this can't be ignored. This is not about turning you into a technologist. It's about helping you become an AI-ready manager—someone who understands what AI is (and isn't), where it fits in real work, and how to guide a team to use it wisely.

Rather than starting with theory alone, the book is grounded in real-world scenarios—across operations, healthcare, education, nonprofits, retail, and more—where managers are experimenting, learning, and sometimes struggling to integrate AI. These are not polished success stories, but practical, imperfect realities shaped by competing priorities, limited time, and constant change.

A central idea runs through every chapter: AI is not a replacement for management—it is an amplifier of it. It can summarize, draft, analyze, and surface insights at remarkable speed, but it cannot replace judgment, context, relationships, or leadership. Those remain firmly human. The managers who thrive will be those who pair their expertise with AI effectively.

Becoming AI-ready is less about tools and more about mindset. It calls for curiosity over fear, experimentation over perfection, and clarity over hype. It means learning to ask better questions, evaluate outputs, and integrate AI into workflows responsibly and in alignment with organizational values—while also guiding your team through the same transition.

This book is an invitation to engage thoughtfully with a shift already underway. You don't need to master everything at once or get it perfect. You simply need to begin—testing, learning, adjusting, and growing more confident over time.

The future of management won't be defined by AI alone, but by managers who know how to use it well.

Introduction to the Book

For years, managers have been told that technology would "change everything." Most of the time, the changes arrived gradually: a new software platform, a better reporting system, a faster way to communicate. Work evolved, but the core experience of management remained familiar. Then artificial intelligence arrived in a different way. Not as another background system, but as something interactive, accessible, and surprisingly capable. Suddenly, a manager could ask a tool to summarize a hundred emails, analyze trends in sales data, draft a proposal, identify risks in a contract, or brainstorm solutions to a staffing problem—all in seconds.

That shift has created both excitement and uncertainty.

Some managers see AI as a powerful advantage. Others see it as confusing, overhyped, or even threatening. Many are caught somewhere in between. They hear bold predictions about the future of work while also watching employees misuse AI to cut corners or generate mediocre output. They experiment with tools only to receive generic responses that feel disconnected from reality. They wonder whether AI is truly useful, whether it can be trusted, and whether learning it is worth the effort.

This book was written for that middle space—not as a technical manual, but as a practical guide for managers navigating the age of AI. You do not need a background in coding, data science, or machine learning to understand it. In fact, one of the biggest misconceptions about AI is that only "tech people" can benefit from it. The truth is that AI is increasingly becoming a management tool. Like email, spreadsheets, or search engines before it, it is moving into the daily flow of work across industries: healthcare, retail, nonprofits, education, logistics, hospitality, manufacturing, government, and nearly every field in between. Throughout this book, you will meet managers facing very real situations:

- A legal advisor reviewing risky vendor contracts
- A nonprofit leader navigating multilingual communication
- A warehouse manager frustrated by poor AI responses
- A school principal trying to overcome teacher skepticism
- A risk manager implementing AI policies
- A marketing director using AI to analyze meeting patterns
- A people analytics leader identifying bias in hiring systems

These examples are intentionally practical. AI becomes much easier to understand when it is connected to actual work rather than abstract theory. The goal is not to impress you with futuristic possibilities. The goal is to help you recognize where AI is already reshaping management and how you can respond wisely.

You will also notice a recurring theme throughout the book: successful AI adoption is often less about technology and more about people. Fear, curiosity, trust, resistance, confidence, and communication all shape whether AI becomes helpful or harmful inside an organization. Managers play a critical role in creating that culture. Employees look to leaders not only for technical direction, but for emotional cues about whether change is safe, useful, and aligned with organizational values.

That means becoming AI-ready is not simply about learning new tools. It is about developing a new kind of managerial literacy. A manager who is AI-ready understands enough to experiment intelligently, guide conversations responsibly, avoid common pitfalls, and help teams focus on practical value instead of distraction. They know how to separate meaningful innovation from shiny noise.

This is especially important because AI is not standing still. The tools described in this book will continue evolving. New platforms will appear. Existing capabilities will improve dramatically. But the deeper principles behind effective adoption—clarity, critical thinking, responsible experimentation, and human-centered leadership—will remain relevant long after today's tools have changed.

In many ways, managers today are standing where leaders once stood during the arrival of the internet, smartphones, or cloud computing. Some dismissed those changes until they were unavoidable. Others chased every trend without a strategy. The most effective leaders learned steadily, adapted thoughtfully, and helped their organizations move forward without panic.

That same opportunity now stands before you.

You do not need to become an AI expert overnight. You do not need to have all the answers. You simply need the willingness to learn, experiment, and lead with wisdom in a changing environment.

Who Can Benefit From This Book?

While the examples in this book span many industries, the core audience is managers and organizational leaders who are responsible for helping people, processes, and decisions move forward in an increasingly AI-shaped world. This book will be especially valuable for:

- **Frontline Managers** who supervise teams and want practical ways to use AI to save time, improve communication, and support better decision-making.
- **Mid-Level Managers and Directors** responsible for operations, projects, staffing, customer experience, analytics, or organizational performance.
- **Senior Leaders and Executives** seeking to understand how AI is affecting management, culture, workflows, and strategic planning across the organization.
- **Project Managers and Scrum Masters** looking for ways to improve planning, collaboration, documentation, and change adoption.
- **HR, Talent Acquisition, and People Analytics Leaders** navigating AI's growing role in hiring, onboarding, retention, and workforce planning.
- **Operations Managers** responsible for logistics, retail, hospitality, manufacturing, healthcare operations, or service delivery.
- **Nonprofit and Ministry Leaders** who want to responsibly explore AI tools while remaining mission-focused and people-centered.

- **Education Leaders and School Administrators** working through both the opportunities and tensions AI creates in learning environments.
- **Risk Management, Legal, and Compliance Professionals** developing policies and safeguards around AI usage.
- **Managers Who Feel Behind Technologically** and need a practical, approachable entry point without technical jargon or coding expertise.
- **Managers Who Are Skeptical of AI** but want to better understand what is real, what is hype, and how AI can be used responsibly.
- **Early AI Adopters** who are experimenting with tools already but want stronger frameworks for implementation, leadership, and team adoption.

This book is also helpful for organizations trying to build a healthier culture around AI adoption. Leaders can use the concepts and case studies in this book to create more thoughtful conversations, stronger policies, and more practical approaches to implementation.

Perhaps most importantly, this book is for managers who understand that leadership is still deeply human work. AI may change how information is processed, how workflows operate, and how quickly tasks are completed—but people still need wisdom, trust, discernment, communication, and vision from their leaders. Managers who learn how to combine those human strengths with the thoughtful use of AI will be better prepared for the future of work.

How to Use This Book

Welcome to your AI navigation journey. This book is designed to be both a roadmap and a companion. It is something you can read cover-to-cover or reference when you need specific directions for where you're headed.

Throughout the book, you'll notice GPS-style navigation markers (📍 🗺 🚗 🎯) displayed at the beginning of each chapter. These markers show exactly where you are in the journey—much like the navigation app on your phone. At any moment, you'll be able to identify your current location, understand the next step, and see how each section connects to the larger route.

Your Dashboard Zones

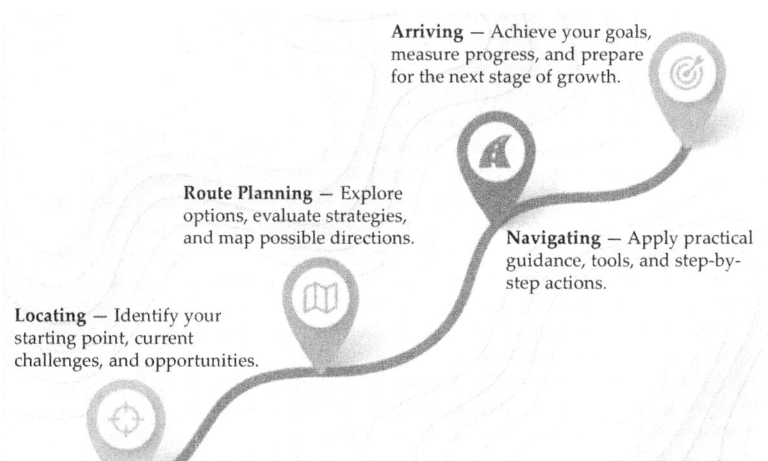

You don't have to rush through this journey. Some managers may move through the entire book in a few weeks, while others may spend more time in the early stages, exploring possibilities and evaluating different paths before choosing a direction. Both approaches get you to the same destination, and both lead toward meaningful progress.

A Note Before We Begin

You might be feeling skeptical. ("*Another thing I'm supposed to learn?*"), or anxious. ("*What if I can't keep up?*"), or even excited but uncertain about where to start. All of those reactions are valid. And all of them are addressed in this book.

The truth is, you already have the hardest skills: you know how to manage people, navigate complexity, and make decisions with incomplete information. AI is just a new tool in your toolkit—and arguably, one of the most powerful you'll ever use. So let's start exploring.

PART 1

Understanding AI Without the Jargon

Before you can use AI effectively, you need a clear understanding of what it actually is—stripped of hype, fear, and unnecessary technical complexity.

In line with the GPS-style navigation system used throughout this book, this is your 📍 Locating phase. Before any route is planned or followed, you first need to identify your starting point. Just as a navigation app first fixes your position on the map, Part 1 helps you understand where you are standing in relation to AI.

It does this by:

- Explaining what AI actually is in plain, accessible language
- Clearing up common myths that often misguide early decisions
- Showing where AI is already present in your everyday work environment
- Setting the mindset needed to navigate the rest of the journey effectively

By the end of Part 1, you will be able to explain AI clearly to your team, recognize real opportunities to use it in your work, and approach new tools with confidence rather than uncertainty—all from a clearly defined starting point on your GPS dashboard.

Chapter 1

What AI Really Is (and Isn't)

1.1 Simple Definition of AI

Let's start with what AI actually means: *Artificial Intelligence (AI) is technology that can learn from data, recognize patterns, and make predictions or decisions without being explicitly programmed for every single scenario.*

Think of it this way: Traditional software is like a recipe. You tell the computer exactly what to do, step by step. "If the user clicks this button, do that. If they enter a number greater than 100, show this error message." Every possibility must be anticipated and coded.

However, AI is different. AI is more like teaching someone how to cook. You show it thousands of examples—"this is what good pasta looks like, this is overcooked, this is undercooked"—and it learns to recognize patterns. Then, when it sees something new, it can make an educated guess based on what it has learned.

When you use AI in your work, you're essentially using a system that has been trained on massive amounts of information and can now:

- **Recognize patterns** you might miss (e.g., spotting trends in customer feedback across thousands of comments)
- **Generate content** based on examples it's seen (e.g., drafting an email in your company's style)
- **Make predictions** based on historical data (e.g., forecasting which projects are most likely to go over budget)

- **Process information** faster than any human could (e.g., summarizing a 50-page report in seconds)

Here's what's crucial to understand: AI doesn't "understand" in the way humans do. When an AI tool writes you a paragraph about project management, it's not drawing from lived experience or genuine comprehension. It's generating text based on patterns it has learned from millions of documents. It's incredibly good at this, sometimes startlingly so, but it's still pattern matching, not actual thinking.

This distinction matters because it shapes how you should use AI. It performs exceptionally well when working with patterns, predictions, and large volumes of information. At the same time, it cannot replace human judgment, experience-driven creativity, or the deeper contextual understanding that only you have about your team, your company culture, and your specific situation.

As a manager, the best way to think about AI is as an incredibly fast, tireless assistant with an extraordinary memory—one that can support decision-making and productivity, but still depends on you for direction, context, and final judgment.

With that perspective in mind, let's address some common myths that often prevent managers from using AI effectively.

1.2 Common Myths Debunked

Now let's clear up some misconceptions that might be holding you back from using AI effectively.

Locating

Myth #1: "AI will replace my job."

Reality: AI replaces tasks, not jobs. And specifically, it replaces the tedious, time-consuming parts of your job you probably don't enjoy anyway.

Will AI draft the first version of your weekly team update? Yes. Will it manage the relationship with an underperforming employee, navigate the politics of a cross-departmental project, or make the final decision to discontinue a struggling initiative? No. Management is fundamentally rooted in human judgment, interpersonal relationships, and context—things AI can *support* but never replace.

Myth #2: "You need a technical background to use AI."

Reality: Using AI tools today is easier than learning to use Microsoft® Excel or PowerPoint was 20 years ago.

Most AI tools now have conversational interfaces. You literally just type what you want in simple language: "Summarize this document and highlight the key risks" or "Draft an email declining this meeting request politely." No coding is required, and in most cases, no specialized technical training is needed. If you can search for information online, you already have the basic skills needed to start using AI. The learning curve isn't technical knowledge; it's learning which tasks to delegate to AI and how to prompt it effectively.

Myth #3: "AI is always right."

Reality: AI often makes mistakes, and that is exactly why human oversight remains essential.

AI generates responses based on patterns, and sometimes those patterns lead to mistakes. It might give you outdated information, make up statistics that sound plausible, or miss crucial nuances in your situation. This is why you should never blindly trust any AI output. Think of it like receiving work from a very fast, confident intern who occasionally makes errors. You review, fact-check, add context, and make the final decision. In other words, AI is not replacing your judgment; it is enhancing your ability to apply it more effectively.

Myth #4: "AI is too expensive for small teams."

Reality: Many powerful AI tools are free or cost less than a typical monthly coffee budget.

Several widely used AI platforms already offer free access or are included in tools organizations use every day. ChatGPT has a free tier. Google's Gemini is free. Microsoft® Copilot comes with many Office 365 subscriptions you probably already have. Additionally, numerous AI productivity tools offer generous free plans. While premium versions exist, you can get substantial value without spending a cent. Even paid tools typically cost $20-30 per month per user, often far less than other workplace software subscriptions. The challenge isn't the cost; it's learning how to integrate AI into everyday workflows smoothly.

Myth #5: "AI will make everything impersonal and robotic."

Reality: AI can actually help managers become more present and engaged with their teams.

When AI handles your routine email responses, document summaries, and data analysis, what are you doing with that reclaimed time? That time can then be invested in having meaningful conversations, coaching employees, solving complex problems, and thinking more strategically about the organization's future. Ironically, the managers who are most concerned about AI making their work feel robotic are often the ones spending hours on tasks that already feel impersonal. AI helps remove much of that operational burden, allowing managers to focus on the aspects of leadership that truly matter.

Myth #6: "If I wait, better AI tools will come along."

Reality: Waiting to adopt AI is like waiting for the «perfect time" to start exercising—there isn't one.

Yes, AI is evolving and improving rapidly. But the skills you build using today's tools will transfer to tomorrow's versions. More importantly, your competitors and peers aren't waiting. The managers who start experimenting now, even imperfectly, are building an advantage that compounds over time. They're learning what works, what doesn't, and how to integrate AI into their workflow. They'll be ready when the next wave of tools arrives. You do not need to wait for the "perfect" AI tool before getting started. The real advantage comes from building familiarity, confidence, and adaptability now so you are prepared for whatever comes next.

Before looking ahead to the future of AI, it is worth recognizing how present it already is in your daily workflow.

1.3 Where AI Is Already Being Used in Everyday Work

Many managers still think AI adoption is something that lies ahead. In reality, AI is already built into many of the tools and platforms professionals use every day, often so seamlessly that its presence goes unnoticed.

In Your Email

Gmail's Smart Compose suggests how to complete your sentences as you type, and Outlook's predictive text works in a similar way. Both use AI trained on large volumes of email data to anticipate what you're likely to write next. The automatic sorting of emails into categories is also AI, as is the spam filter that keeps your inbox clean by identifying unwanted messages through pattern recognition.

Manager's Moment

On a Tuesday morning, a regional operations manager at a mid-sized nonprofit began the day with a familiar problem: too many emails and not enough clarity. Overnight, her inbox was filled with updates from field teams across five states. Instead of responding to them in the order they came in, she dropped the messages into ChatGPT with the prompt:

"Act as a regional operations manager. I will paste a series of emails from field teams.

Summarize the content into a structured briefing with the following sections:

1. Top 5 priorities (ranked by urgency)
2. Key themes or patterns across teams
3. Recurring issues or bottlenecks
4. Items that require my decision or follow-up

Keep the summary concise, use bullet points, and highlight anything that appears more than once across different emails."

Within seconds, she had a clean briefing about her priorities for the day. One thread flagged a recurring delay in volunteer onboarding. Another highlighted confusion around a new reporting process. The AI didn't fix the issues, but it quickly pulled together insights that would normally take over an hour to compile manually.

In Your Meetings

If you've used Zoom's automatic transcription, Microsoft® Teams' meeting summaries, or Google Meet's real-time captions, you've used AI. These tools process spoken language in real-time, convert it to text, identify speakers, and even highlight key moments or action items. Some managers are now using tools like Otter.ai or Fireflies.ai that not only transcribe meetings but automatically generate summaries, extract action items, and even answer questions about what was discussed.

In Your Analytics

Look at any dashboard in your business intelligence tools—Salesforce, Tableau, Microsoft® Power BI. Those "insights" and "anomaly detection" features are powered by AI analyzing your data to surface patterns you might otherwise miss. When your CRM suggests which leads are most likely to convert, that's predictive AI. When your financial software flags unusual spending patterns, that's AI-powered risk assessment.

Manager's Moment

The Director of Programs at a workforce development nonprofit was preparing for his monthly check-in with the executive director. Staring at a dense Microsoft® Excel spreadsheet full of placement rates, retention numbers, and training completion stats, he couldn't identify the most important themes to share with his boss.

> He opened Microsoft® Copilot and typed the following prompt:
>
> "Analyze the data in this spreadsheet, and give me the key themes from the data. Use the thresholds of 80% (acceptable) and 50% (below expectations) to identify placement rates, retention rates and training completion rates that are out of standard. Recommend what I should talk to my boss about in my monthly check-in meeting. Format your response as an executive summary."
>
> Microsoft® Copilot returned a pretty good summary, but he had to ask it to remove flowery and overly optimistic language before he was satisfied that it was presentable to his boss. He had Microsoft® Copilot export the report to a Word document that he could print and take with him to his meeting.

In Your Content Creation

Whether you know it or not, AI is probably helping you write. Tools like Grammarly use AI to suggest corrections and improvements. Many content management systems now include AI-powered writing assistants. LinkedIn's post suggestions are powered by AI analyzing what content performs best. Even your phone's autocorrect has evolved into predictive AI that adapts to your writing style over time.

In Your Customer Service

If your company has a chatbot on its website, automated email responses, or intelligent routing of support tickets, you're using AI. These systems are handling routine inquiries, categorizing issues, and directing customers to the right resources—all without human intervention for standard questions.

The point isn't that you need to use all these tools. The point is that AI is already woven into your work environment. You're probably benefiting from it already in small ways. This chapter simply makes that invisible help visible, so you can be more intentional about using it.

Try This Week

Pick one tool you already use (email, calendar, or a meeting platform) awnd explore its AI features. Spend 15 minutes reviewing its capabilities or watching a quick tutorial to understand how AI is already built into your workflow and how you can start using it more intentionally.

When You're Ready

Keep a simple log for three days: every time you notice yourself doing a repetitive task like drafting similar emails, summarizing information, searching for data, write it down. These are your prime candidates for AI assistance.

CHAPTER 2

Developing an AI Mindset

Understanding what AI is gives you knowledge, but knowledge alone doesn't drive adoption. What separates managers who successfully integrate AI from those who struggle to get started is mindset—the mental frameworks through which they approach and use this technology.

This chapter isn't about technical skills. It focuses on three mindset shifts: approaching AI with curiosity instead of fear, balancing efficiency with ethical responsibility, and staying adaptable as technology keeps changing. Get these right, and AI adoption becomes a natural part of how you work.

2.1 Embracing Curiosity Over Fear

Let's acknowledge the elephant in the room: AI can feel threatening to many managers. Will it replace me? Will I look incompetent if I don't understand it? What if I make a mistake using it?

These fears are understandable, but they're also a trap. The managers using AI aren't fearless—they're just curious. They've shifted from asking *"What could go wrong?"* to *"What could I learn?"* That small reframing changes everything.

Fear tends to make us defensive. It leads to hesitation, avoidance of experimentation, and a preference for waiting until others figure things out first. In that state, uncertainty can cloud judgment and cause us to miss valuable opportunities. Curiosity, on the other hand, makes you proactive.

It encourages action, even in small steps. You try things, observe what happens, and build confidence through experience rather than waiting for certainty to arrive.

Think about the last time you learned a new skill—maybe it was using a new software platform, picking up a management framework, or adapting to a company reorganization. Success rarely came from having everything figured out in advance. It came from experimenting, asking questions, making mistakes, and continuing to move forward.

AI is no different. You don't need to master it before you start. You need to be curious enough to try. Let's look at practical ways to build that curiosity.

Practical Ways to Cultivate Curiosity

- **Start small and specific.** Don't try to "learn AI." Instead, pick one task you do regularly and ask: "Could AI help with this?" Then test it. Give yourself permission to fail. Your first attempts will be clunky. Your prompts won't be perfect. You'll get weird outputs. That's not failure—that's learning.
- **Ask "why" and "how" questions.** When you see an AI tool in action, don't just accept it. Ask: Why did it give that answer? How might I improve this prompt? What pattern is it recognizing? This turns passive consumption into active learning.
- **Share what you discover.** Curiosity compounds when it's social. Tell a colleague about something you tried. Join a conversation about AI tools in your industry. Teaching others what you're learning reinforces your own understanding and keeps you engaged.

The goal isn't to become an AI expert. The goal is to build a mindset where learning about AI feels like an opportunity, not an obligation.

Manager's Moment

A communications manager had built her reputation on being thorough, thoughtful, and precise with words. She took pride in crafting messages that were well received even when the topic was unpopular. When her organization began encouraging the use of AI tools, she felt a quiet resistance rise up. If a machine could draft emails, summarize reports, and generate content in seconds, what did that mean for the value she had spent years developing? She avoided the tools at first, telling herself they were overhyped. But underneath, there was a more honest concern: *If this works, where does that leave me?*

During a team meeting, a colleague casually said, "I've been using AI as a first draft partner…it's not perfect, but it gets me unstuck." That one comment changed her mindset, and she decided to do a small experiment. She opened her company's Claude account and asked it to give her a rough outline for a company-wide communication about changes to the benefit enrollment process. She told Claude what the major changes were and how these would impact the employees' coverage and financial contributions. It returned an outline that was a good starting point for her communication, but because it was just an outline, she could still use her writing skills to craft the message. She was grateful that it suggested addressing potential resistance to the increased employee contribution. She then used Claude to help frame her message in a way that reduced the likelihood of a negative reaction. After this experience, she understood that AI wasn't a threat, but an

> opportunity to make her writing process faster and more effective.

2.2 Balancing Efficiency With Ethics

AI offers a powerful promise: doing more in less time and improving decision-making at scale. Yet when efficiency goes unchecked, it can introduce risks that quietly affect teams and outcomes. The managers who use AI most effectively aren't the ones who maximize efficiency at all costs. They're the ones who balance speed with responsibility.

The core tension is simple but important: AI can work faster than any human, but it can also produce biased, inaccurate, or sensitive outputs if not handled carefully. As a manager, your responsibility goes beyond usage; it extends to responsible application. Let's explore what that looks like in practice.

Bias Is Baked into AI Systems

AI learns from data, and data reflects the world, including its inequities. If you use AI for hiring and the training data reflects historical bias (like favoring men more than women in leadership roles), the AI will likely perpetuate that bias. This doesn't mean you can't use AI for hiring. It means you need to be aware, actively test outputs, and maintain human oversight on final decisions.

Privacy Matters More Than Efficiency

Before you feed customer data, employee information, or proprietary documents into an AI tool, ask:

- Where is this data going?
- Who has access to it?
- What are the terms of service?

Some AI tools learn from the inputs you provide, which means your sensitive information could be retained or exposed. It's important to always review policies carefully and use enterprise-grade tools with appropriate data protections when handling confidential information. Never trade privacy for convenience.

Transparency Builds Trust

If you're using AI to draft communications, analyze performance data, or make recommendations, your team deserves to know. Not because AI use is something to hide, but because hidden automation can erode trust. A simple approach is to be open about what is being automated and where human judgment still plays a central role. For example, stating, "I used AI to summarize these reports so we can focus on the decisions only we can make," is an open approach that reinforces trust and confidence.

Human Judgment Remains Non-Negotiable

AI should inform decisions, not make them. This is especially critical for anything involving people—performance reviews, promotions, terminations, or conflict resolution. AI can identify patterns, organize data, or draft initial thoughts, but the final decision must *always* rest with you.

Manager's Moment

A finance manager at a large oil and gas company thought AI might be a big time-saver for preparing the quarterly report. He uploaded the financial projections and results from each of the regions to Gemini and asked it to create a Microsoft® PowerPoint slide deck for the quarterly update with the senior

> executives. The results were impressive and highly insightful. He then refined it with a few corrections and improvements.
>
> He met his Director a few days later and excitedly told her how Gemini had saved him hours in preparing for the meeting. He didn't get the reaction he expected. His Director was shocked that he had uploaded the company's proprietary financial data into an AI tool. She reprimanded him for putting the company at risk by sharing confidential data and told him to never do that again.
>
> The finance manager's excitement turned to embarrassment. To make matters worse, his Director told him that the company had a policy governing the types of data that could be uploaded to AI tools. He spent the next hour reviewing the definitions of Class 1 (Restricted), Class 2 (Sensitive), and Class 3 (Public) data.

Before using AI for any task, ask three questions:

- Could this harm someone if it's wrong? (If yes, increase human oversight)
- Does this involve sensitive or private information? (If yes, verify data handling)
- Will people know AI was involved? (If yes, disclose it clearly)

Efficiency is valuable, but trust, fairness, and ethical responsibility are irreplaceable. The best managers design AI use in a way that strengthens both productivity and responsibility.

2.3 Staying Adaptable in a Shifting Tech Landscape

Managers must face an uncomfortable truth: the AI tools you learn today may look very different—or even become obsolete—within a couple of years. New capabilities emerge constantly and what seemed impossible just months ago can quickly become standard practice. The landscape doesn't just shift; it accelerates.

This can feel unsettling. "Why invest time learning something that will soon change?" But that question misses the point. The goal is not to master individual tools; it is to build adaptability: the mindset and skills that allow you to navigate constant change with confidence, no matter what comes next.

Adaptability Starts With Principles, Not Tools

When you understand the underlying principles of how AI works and where it adds value, you can quickly assess new tools without starting from scratch. You don't need to relearn everything when ChatGPT releases a new version or a competitor launches a better product. You evaluate it through your existing framework: What problem does this solve? Where does it fit in my workflow? What are the risks?

Embrace "Good Enough for Now"

Perfectionism is the enemy of adaptability. Managers who wait for the definitive guide, the perfect tool, or complete mastery before adopting AI will always be behind. Instead, adopt a "good enough for now" approach. Use what is available today, learn what works in practice, and refine as you go. When better options emerge, adjust accordingly.

Build Learning into Your Routine

Staying current doesn't mean reading every AI headline or chasing every new release. It means creating small, sustainable habits. Set aside 15 minutes weekly to scan AI developments in your industry. Follow two or three trusted sources. Join one community where managers share practical applications. The goal isn't to know everything; it's to maintain enough awareness to identify and act on opportunities early.

Experiment in Low-Stakes Environments

Managers who adapt fastest are the ones who experiment regularly—not through big, risky bets, but through small, reversible tests. Try a new AI tool for a personal task before introducing it to your team. Experiment with different prompts to see what works. Treat AI like a laboratory where failure is feedback, not consequence. This builds pattern recognition and confidence that transfer across tools.

Manager's Moment

Ethan, a Senior Manager, had spent fifteen years in operations, building systems that ran on precision and predictability. When AI tools started showing up in meetings and inboxes, he kept his distance. It wasn't just skepticism—it was the frustration of feeling like a beginner again. The turning point came when a colleague suggested something simple: "Why don't you ask the AI to teach you?" That felt different. Instead of trying to master a new tool all at once, Ethan opened a blank chat and typed, "Explain how I can use AI in my role as an operations manager. Start simple and give me one small task to try." The response didn't overwhelm him. It gave him a single step—use AI to summarize a weekly operations report—and even included the exact prompt to copy and paste. That small win shifted everything.

> Ethan went back and asked, "What's the next step?" and then, "How can I improve my prompt?" The AI became less like a tool he had to figure out and more like a coach that met him where he was. Within a few weeks, he was using it to draft process updates, analyze recurring issues, and prepare for team meetings. Most importantly, his mindset changed. He no longer saw AI as something to catch up to, but something he could learn alongside. By letting the technology teach him how to use it, he removed the pressure to be an expert before he interacted with the tool.

The bottom line is that the landscape will continue to shift. Your job isn't to predict every change; it's to build the mindset that makes you ready for whatever comes next.

Try This Week

Identify one task where you're letting fear (of making mistakes, looking incompetent, or disrupting your routine) prevent you from trying AI. Name the fear specifically. Then ask yourself: "What's the smallest, safest experiment I could run to test this?" Take that step, even if it's just five minutes with a free tool.

When You're Ready

Create a personal "AI Ethics Checklist" with three questions you will ask before using AI for any significant task. Ground it in your own values and your team's needs. Keep it visible, and refer to it regularly in your day-to-day work. This simple tool will quietly guide many of your future decisions.

PART 2

Practical AI Use Cases for Managers

Here is where theory becomes practice. Over the next three chapters, you'll move from understanding AI to actually using it in your daily work. Each section includes real tools, practical prompts, and step-by-step guidance designed for immediate application.

Continuing the GPS analogy, this is your Route Planning phase. A navigation system doesn't offer just one path—it presents multiple routes depending on your destination and priorities. Part 2 does the same, mapping out three practical directions that address common managerial challenges:

- **Route 1:** Personal productivity (scheduling, writing, information processing)
- **Route 2:** Team collaboration (meetings, communication, brainstorming)
- **Route 3:** Strategic decisions (analytics, forecasting, risk assessment)

Don't take all routes at once. You choose one, navigate it successfully, and then expand to the others as your confidence grows. This phase is about direction, not speed—choosing a path, following it clearly, and building momentum step by step.

Chapter 3

Personal Productivity Boosters

Before you can champion AI adoption with your team, you need to experience its value firsthand. This chapter focuses on three high-impact areas where AI can improve your personal productivity: managing your time and priorities, accelerating your writing, and processing information faster.

3.1 Scheduling, Prioritization, and Note-Taking

You start each day with clear intentions and a well-defined plan. But as the day unfolds, emails start piling up, meetings run longer than expected, and urgent requests keep shifting your attention. Before you know it, it's 4 PM, and the most important work you planned is still waiting. Does this sound familiar?

This is not a time-management failure; it's a reality of modern management work. AI can't create more hours in your day, but it can help you use the hours you have more intelligently. Here's how:

3.1.1 Smart Scheduling With AI

Coordinating meetings across multiple calendars, time zones, and packed schedules can quickly become a productivity drain. What should be a simple 30-minute discussion often turns into a chain of emails. AI-powered tools such as Clockwise, Reclaim.ai, and Microsoft® Copilot's scheduling assistant reduce this friction by automatically suggesting optimal meeting slots based on your availability and work patterns.

Tool Example #1: Clockwise

Clockwise integrates with Google Calendar or Outlook and uses AI to automatically reschedule flexible meetings, creating uninterrupted blocks of "Focus Time." It adapts to your work patterns—such as peak productivity hours and typical task durations—and optimizes your calendar accordingly. Many users report gaining 3–5 hours of focused work time per week within the first month.

How to set it up:

- Connect your calendar (Google or Outlook)
- Set your "Focus Time" preferences (e.g., "I need 2-hour blocks on Tuesday and Thursday mornings")
- Identify which meetings are flexible and which are fixed
- Let Clockwise's AI reorganize your schedule

Tool Example #2: Motion

Motion is an AI-powered combination of a project manager and calendar. You input your tasks, deadlines, and priorities, and it automatically schedules when you should work on each item based on urgency, available time, and your productivity patterns. Instead of manually deciding when to do what, Motion handles the "Tetris" of your day for you.

How it works:

- Add your tasks with deadlines and estimated time requirements
- Motion's AI analyzes your calendar
- It automatically schedules tasks into your day, shifting them around meetings
- As priorities change or new meetings are added, Motion automatically reschedules your plan in real time

3.1.2 AI-Powered Prioritization

When you're managing 50+ tasks and everything feels urgent, it becomes difficult to know where to begin. AI tools such as Trevor AI, Sunsama, and TimeHero help you prioritize based on deadlines, task dependencies, workload, and even patterns from how you typically manage similar work.

Even without specialized tools, you can use ChatGPT for prioritization. Here's a prompt that works:

> I have these tasks this week:
>
> 1. [List your tasks with context]
> 2. [Include deadlines and rough time estimates]
> 3. [Note any dependencies]
>
> Help me prioritize these using the Eisenhower Matrix (urgent/important).
>
> For each task, explain your reasoning and suggest when I should tackle it this week.

AI can assess urgency and importance more objectively, without the emotional attachment we often bring to tasks. It also encourages clarity by requiring deadlines, effort estimates, and dependencies.

3.1.3 Intelligent Note-Taking

You take notes during meetings, but they often end up scattered across notebooks, documents, or apps, making them difficult to search and even harder to turn into action. AI-powered note-taking tools go beyond simple transcription by organizing information, generating summaries, and automatically identifying action items.

Tool Example: Notion AI

If you already use Notion for documentation, Notion AI can turn rough meeting notes into structured summaries, extract action items, and even suggest follow-up questions worth exploring.

How to use it:

- During or after a meeting, paste your rough notes into a Notion page
- Highlight the text and select "Ask AI" → "Summarize"
- Use "Find action items" to automatically create a checklist
- Use "Improve writing" to turn fragmented notes into clear documentation

Table 3.1 Converting Rough Notes into Actionable Summaries

Before AI:	After Notion AI (Summary + Action Items):
meeting w/ sarah about Q2 goals - she mentioned budget concerns, wants to shift resources to digital, timeline pushed to end of april, need to follow up with finance team	**Meeting Summary:** Discussed Q2 goals with Sarah. Key points: - Budget concerns require resource reallocation - Strategic shift toward digital initiatives - Timeline extended to April 30th
	Action Items: - [ ] Follow up with finance team on budget reallocation - [ ] Draft revised Q2 timeline for Sarah's review - [ ] Identify resources available for digital initiatives

Manager's Moment

Lena, a Project Manager, was leading a complex organizational redesign—new roles, shifting reporting lines, updated workflows—and her tasks kept multiplying by the hour. Instead of juggling spreadsheets, documents, and scattered notes, she built a central workspace in Notion. Each workstream had its own page, with tasks, owners, and timelines linked together. But the real shift came when she began using Notion AI inside those pages. After long stakeholder meetings, she would paste her notes and ask the AI to extract action items, assign owners based on context, and flag dependencies she might have missed.

As the redesign progressed, Lena relied on the AI to keep everything moving. She used it to generate weekly status updates, summarize risks across teams, and even draft communication plans for leaders navigating change. The outputs weren't final, but they were fast and structured—giving her something solid to refine rather than starting from scratch each time. More importantly, she stopped feeling buried in coordination work and began seeing the whole system more clearly. By pairing her judgment with AI's ability to organize and surface insights, she was able to stay ahead of her deadlines.

With the right approach, AI becomes more than a tool; it becomes a productivity partner that supports your daily work.

3.2 Drafting Emails and Reports Faster

Writing takes up a massive portion of your day—emails, status reports, project updates, performance reviews, policy documents. What if you could cut that time in half without sacrificing quality?

3.2.1 The AI Writing Process in Three Stages

Many managers make the mistake of expecting AI to produce a polished final product immediately. When the result feels generic, they assume, "AI doesn't understand my work."
In reality, the greatest value often comes from using AI to create a strong first draft and then refining it with your own expertise, judgment, tone, and voice. Figure 3.1 illustrates a simple three-stage workflow for collaborating effectively with AI.

Figure 3.1 **Stages of An Effective Ai-Assisted Workflow**

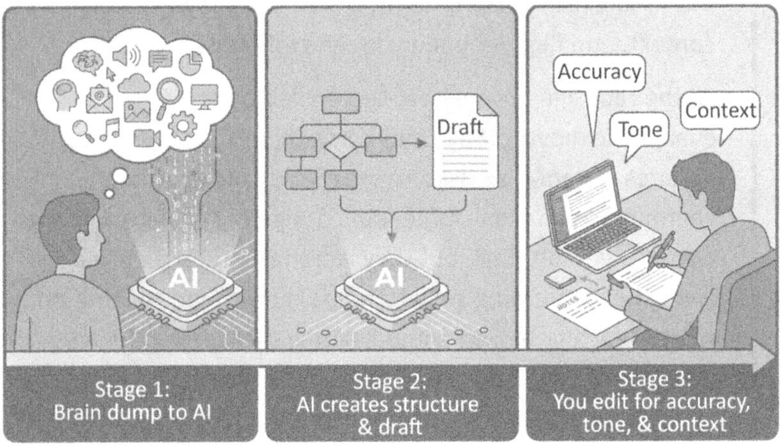

AI Tool: Google Gemini

Prompt: Generate a visual illustrating the three stages of an effective AI-assisted workflow.

Let's explore how these stages apply through a few scenarios:

Scenario 1: Drafting emails with AI

You need to decline a meeting request without damaging the relationship. Traditionally, you might stare at a blank email, write and rewrite multiple drafts, and still feel unsatisfied with the final version after spending 15–20 minutes on it.

Instead, you can use a simple prompt to create a strong first draft in seconds:

> Write a professional email declining a meeting invitation.
>
> Context:
>
> - The meeting is about a cross-functional project I'm not directly involved in
> - I want to maintain a positive relationship with the organizer
> - I'd be happy to provide input asynchronously or nominate someone from my team
> - Tone should be warm but clear
>
> Keep it under 100 words.

AI output

> Hi [Name],
>
> Thanks for thinking of me for this discussion. While I'd love to contribute, I'm not directly involved enough in this project to add meaningful value to a live meeting.
>
> Would it help if I provided input asynchronously, or I can connect you with [Team Member Name] who has more context on this area?
>
> Happy to support however is most useful.
>
> Best,
>
> [Your Name]

Your edit (30 seconds):

- Replace [Name] and [Team Member Name]
- Maybe adjust one phrase to match your voice

Scenario 2: Weekly status report

You need to write a weekly status report for your leadership team, highlighting key updates. Here's a prompt you can use to generate the report quickly:

> Write a weekly status report for my leadership team.
>
> **Key updates:**
>
> - Launched new customer portal (3 days early)
> - Onboarded two new team members
> - Database migration delayed to next week due to a vendor issue
> - Team morale is high, several people mentioned appreciating the new flexible schedule
>
> **Format:** Brief bullet points. Professional but not stiff. Highlight the portal launch as the main win.

AI output

> **Weekly Highlights**
>
> **Big Win:** New customer portal launched 3 days ahead of schedule. Early feedback from beta users is positive.
>
> **Team Updates:**
>
> - Welcomed [Name] and [Name] to the team—onboarding in progress
> - Team morale remains strong; flexible schedule policy continues to be well-received
>
> **In Progress:**
>
> - Database migration pushed to next week due to vendor delay (no impact on customer experience)
>
> **Next Week Focus:**
>
> - Complete database migration

- Begin portal feature iteration based on user feedback

Your edit (2-5 minutes):

- Add the names
- Adjust the emoji if that's not your style
- Include any additional context

Scenario 3: Drafting reports and documentation

You need to document why a project exceeded its budget and what can be learned from it. Instead of spending hours building the report structure from scratch, let AI handle the initial organization:

Write a project post-mortem report.

Project: Website redesign

Timeline: 6 months (planned), 8 months (actual)

Budget: $150K (planned), $190K (actual)

What went well:

- Final product exceeded stakeholder expectations
- Strong collaboration between design and dev teams
- User testing revealed insights that improved final product

What went wrong:

- Scope creep in months 3-4 (added features not in original spec)
- Vendor deliverables delayed twice (2 weeks, then 3 weeks)
- Underestimated time needed for stakeholder review cycles

Format: Professional project post-mortem. Include sections for Overview, Successes, Challenges, Lessons Learned, and Recommendations.

AI output (condensed)

Project Post-Mortem: Website Redesign

Overview

The website redesign project concluded in Month 8, two months beyond the original timeline, with final costs of $190K against a $150K budget. Despite timeline and budget overruns, the final deliverable exceeded stakeholder expectations and incorporated valuable user insights.

Successes

- Final product quality surpassed initial goals
- Cross-functional collaboration between design and development teams was exemplary
- User testing phase yielded actionable insights that significantly improved the end product

Challenges

- Scope expansion during months 3-4 added unplanned features
- Vendor delays (2 weeks in Month 4, 3 weeks in Month 5) disrupted timeline
- Stakeholder review cycles required more time than anticipated

Lessons Learned

[This is where YOU add the real value - AI can't know your organizational context or strategic implications]

Recommendations

[Again, this is your expertise - AI provides structure, you provide insight]

Your edit (10-15 minutes):

- Specific lessons learned based on your team's experience
- Recommendations that account for your company's processes and politics
- Context about why certain challenges mattered more than others
- Your perspective on what to do differently next time

3.2.2 Essentials of Effective AI Prompting

To get the best results from AI writing tools, it's important to provide clear, structured prompts. Based on these examples, here's a simple formula that consistently works:

- **Specify the format/type** (email, report, memo, etc.)
- **Provide context** (who's the audience, what's the situation)
- **Give key information/facts** (the raw material AI needs)
- **Set tone and length** (professional, warm, concise, under 200 words, etc.)
- **Clarify what to emphasize** (what's most important)

Example

✗ **Bad prompt:** "Write an email about the budget."

☑ **Good prompt:** "Write a professional email to my CFO explaining why our department needs a 15% budget increase. Context: Industry benchmarking shows we're understaffed. Tone: Data-driven but respectful. Length: Under 150 words."

Think of AI as a writing assistant that helps build the scaffolding, while you remain the architect shaping the final outcome. AI can draft the content, but you still need to:

- Add specific details only you know
- Adjust tone to match your voice and relationship with the recipient
- Verify all facts and figures`
- Make final judgment on what to include or exclude

3.3 Summarizing Long Documents in Seconds

Let's look at a scenario: you receive a 45-page proposal from a software vendor. Your team needs a decision by next week. You need to know: What are they proposing? What does it cost? What are the risks? What requires deeper review?

Traditionally, this would mean setting aside 90 minutes or more to read the entire document, take notes, and try to retain the important details.

With AI, the process becomes far more efficient. In about 10 minutes, you can generate a comprehensive summary of the document and then focus your attention on the sections that truly matter. Instead of reading everything line by line, you can move directly into targeted deep dives and decision-making.

3.3.1 Using AI for Document Summarization

Here's a simple process for using AI to summarize documents effectively.

Step 1: Upload or paste the document

Most AI tools now accept PDF uploads. Claude (Anthropic's AI) handles this particularly well, as does ChatGPT Plus. If you're using the free version of ChatGPT, you'll need to copy-paste text in chunks.

Step 2: Use a structured prompt

Summarize this vendor proposal. I need to understand:

1. What they're offering (main features/services)
2. Total cost and payment structure
3. Implementation timeline
4. Key risks or concerns

Keep the summary under 500 words. Use bullet points for clarity.

AI output (condensed)

Vendor Proposal Summary: [Vendor Name]

What They're Offering:

- Cloud-based project management platform with AI-powered analytics
- Includes: task management, resource allocation, real-time reporting, and integration with existing tools (Slack, Microsoft® 365, Salesforce)
- Custom dashboard development and 6 months of dedicated support

Cost Structure:

- Year 1: $85,000 ($60K platform license + $25K implementation)
- Years 2-3: $65,000/year (license + standard support)
- Additional users: $1,200/year per user after first 50
- Total 3-year cost: ~$215,000

Implementation Timeline:

- Weeks 1-4: Discovery and configuration
- Weeks 5-8: Data migration and integration
- Weeks 9-10: User training
- Week 11: Go-live
- Weeks 12-24: Dedicated support period

Key Risks/Concerns:

- Data migration depends on quality of current data (they note "legacy system cleanup may extend timeline")
- Integration with Salesforce marked as "medium complexity" - may require custom development

Step 3: Ask follow-up questions

The real power of AI summarization lies not just in generating an initial summary, but in enabling deeper exploration through targeted follow-up questions, such as:

- "What are the potential hidden costs not explicitly mentioned?"
- "Compare this proposal's pricing to typical industry rates for similar platforms."
- "What questions should I ask during the vendor demo, based on this proposal?"
- "Identify any terminology or technical requirements I should clarify with our IT team."
- "What would a strong counter-proposal look like?"

Every answer is generated in roughly 30 seconds, enabling an interactive conversation with the document through AI.

3.3.2 Using AI for Meeting Notes

Here's another scenario: your colleague attended a two-hour industry conference session and shared 12 pages of notes with you, but you only need the key takeaways. In this case, you could use the following prompt:

> These are notes from a conference session on [topic]. Summarize:
>
> 1. The 3 most important trends or insights
> 2. Any recommendations or best practices mentioned
> 3. Actionable ideas relevant to [your specific area - e.g., "mid-sized companies in healthcare"]
>
> Make it scannable - I need to brief my team in 5 minutes.

Instead of working through pages of scattered notes, AI can quickly produce a focused, actionable summary that highlights the information most relevant to you and your team.

3.3.3 Using AI for Industry Reports and Research

Keeping up with industry trends can be difficult when you do not have time to read every analyst report. One practical solution is to build a monthly routine where you use AI to summarize the most important reports with the following prompt:

> Summarize this [industry] report.
>
> **Focus on:**
>
> - Market trends that could impact our business in the next 12 months
> - Competitive intelligence (what are leading companies doing?)

- Technology shifts we should be aware of
- Any data points or statistics worth noting

Structure: Brief executive summary, then key findings by category.

This approach helps you stay informed while dramatically reducing the time spent reviewing lengthy reports.

Manager's Moment

A senior legal advisor opened a vendor's revised contract with a familiar sense of tension. The partnership had been rocky, and past revisions had a way of burying unfavorable terms deep in dense language. This time, she turned to Claude to help her scan the terrain. She uploaded both the previous version and the new draft, then gave a precise prompt:

"Act as a senior legal analyst. Compare these two versions of a vendor contract and identify any changes that could materially impact our company. Highlight differences in liability, indemnification, termination clauses, pricing, service levels, and dispute resolution. Flag any subtle or potentially hidden changes, summarize risks in plain language, and note anything that deviates from standard industry terms."

Within moments, Claude returned a structured comparison, surfacing a revised indemnification clause (one party agreeing to cover the losses of another party) and a shortened notice of termination—both easy to miss in a document of that size.

Receiving the output, she drilled into the flagged sections, confirming the changes and considering their implications in light of the vendor's history. What might have taken hours of line-by-line comparison became a more focused, strategic review. AI helped her see through the fog of legal language so that she could engage the vendor with clarity and confidence.

3.3.4 What AI Summarization Does Well (and Poorly)

AI is highly effective for certain types of summarization tasks, but there are still areas where human interpretation remains critical.

Table 3.2 Strengths and Limitations of AI Summarization

AI excels at:	AI struggles with:
• Extracting key facts, figures, and main points	• Understanding subtle context or subtext
• Identifying themes across long documents	• Identifying what's politically important in your organization
• Creating structured outlines from unstructured text	• Knowing what *you* specifically care about (unless you tell it)
• Comparing multiple documents for similarities/ differences	• Catching intentional misdirection or biased framing in source material
• Answering specific questions about document content	

Pro Tips for Document Summarization

- **Be specific about what you care about.** "Summarize this" gets generic results. "Summarize this focusing on budget implications and implementation risks" gets insightful results.
- **Use AI to compare documents.** Upload two vendor proposals and ask AI to create a comparison table. Upload your draft and a competitor's approach and ask what yours is missing.

- **Iterate your summary.** If the first summary isn't quite right, refine: "That's good, but make it more focused on operational impact" or "Expand the section on risks."
- **Always verify critical facts.** AI summarization is generally accurate, but for anything you'll act on or share publicly, check key details against the original document.

Instead of drowning in information overload, you can use AI to quickly highlight the insights, risks, and make decisions that matter most.

Try This Week

Pick one of these three areas to experiment with:

Option 1 - Scheduling: Try Clockwise or Reclaim.ai (both have free trials). Connect your calendar and let it run for one week. Observe what changes.

Option 2 - Writing: The next time you need to write an email or short report, use the AI-assisted approach. Time yourself doing it the old way first (mentally), then use AI. Compare the results and time saved.

Option 3 - Summarizing: Find one long document you've been avoiding (report, proposal, meeting notes). Use an AI tool to summarize it. See if the summary gives you what you need.

When You're Ready

- **Create your "AI Writing Prompts" library:** Start a document where you save prompts that work well for your recurring writing tasks (status reports, meeting declines, project updates, etc.). Each time you craft a good prompt, add it to your library. Within a month, you'll have a personal toolkit that saves hours every week.
- **Track your time savings:** For two weeks, note every time you use AI for productivity tasks and estimate time saved. Most managers find they're saving 5-10 hours per week once they build the habit. That's 200-400 hours per year. What would you do with that time?

CHAPTER 4

Team Collaboration and Communication

In Chapter 3, you learned how AI can amplify your personal productivity. Now let's extend that impact to your entire team.

This chapter explores three high-leverage ways AI can improve team dynamics: capturing and acting on meeting insights, breaking down language barriers for global teams, and enhancing collaborative brainstorming.

4.1 AI for Meeting Transcripts and Action Items

Meetings are where collaboration happens—but also where productivity is often lost. The average manager spends 23 hours per week in meetings. If even 30% of that time is wasted on unclear outcomes, forgotten decisions, or lost action items, you're losing nearly 7 hours every week.

AI can't make bad meetings good, but it can ensure that good meetings actually lead to action.

4.1.1 The Meeting Problem AI Solves

How many times has this happened: You have a productive discussion, everyone leaves aligned, and two weeks later someone asks, "Wait, what did we decide about that?" Nobody's quite sure. The meeting notes are scattered or incomplete, so another meeting is spent revisiting the same discussion.

AI meeting tools help eliminate this cycle by automatically capturing conversations, organizing key insights, and creating a searchable record of decisions and action items. Let's look at some tools that improve meeting follow-through:

Tool Example #1: Otter.ai

What it does: Otter.ai joins your video calls on Zoom, Teams, or Google Meet, transcribes conversations in real time, identifies speakers, and generates summaries with action items.

How to use it:

- Connect Otter to your calendar
- It automatically joins scheduled meetings (or you can manually start recording)
- After the meeting, it generates a full transcript, summary, action items, and key topics
- You can search across past meetings (e.g., "What did we decide about the vendor contract?")

Otter.ai can also identify action items automatically. For example, if someone says, "John will send the proposal by Friday," the platform flags it as a task assigned to John with a Friday deadline.

Tool Example #2: Fireflies.ai

Some teams prefer Fireflies.ai because it adds conversation analytics to meeting transcripts. It can track speaking time, identify questions asked, and highlight dominant discussion topics, helping teams improve meeting dynamics over time.

Manager's Moment

A marketing director preparing for a high-stakes product launch had a nagging sense that her weekly project meetings weren't as effective as they could be. They felt busy, but not always productive. To get clarity, she began using Fireflies.ai to record and analyze each meeting over the course of a month. After four sessions, she asked the tool to compare conversation analytics across all meetings: who spoke most, how long topics lingered, how often decisions were made, and where action items were assigned. She observed a pattern: she was speaking 50% of the time while key product and engineering contributors stayed quiet, and the same issues kept repeating.

Armed with that insight, she made a few deliberate changes. She revised the agenda to prioritize decisions first, assigned sections of the meeting to specific team leads, and intentionally paused to draw out quieter voices. She also ended each meeting by having Fireflies.ai generate and review action items live, ensuring accountability before anyone logged off. Within two weeks, the tone of the meetings shifted. Participation broadened, decisions happened faster, and fewer topics carried over from one week to the next. Fireflies.ai gave her clearer visibility into how the meetings were actually functioning, not just how they seemed.

4.1.2 Best Practices for Implementing AI-Powered Meeting Notes

Start with low-stakes meetings. Don't introduce AI transcription in your most sensitive executive session. Start with routine team meetings where everyone's comfortable experimenting.

Set expectations upfront. At the meeting start: "We're using Otter to capture notes and action items. The transcript is for our team only. Is everyone okay with this?" Getting explicit consent builds trust.

Review before sharing. AI is 85-95% accurate, but it makes mistakes, especially with industry jargon, names, or unclear audio. Spend 2 minutes scanning the summary before distributing. Fix obvious errors, clarify ambiguous points.

Create a follow-up ritual. The real value isn't the transcript, it's what you do with it. Establish a pattern: Meeting ends → AI generates summary → You review → Share within 2 hours → Everyone knows their action items before end of day.

4.1.3 Strategic Uses of AI Meeting Transcripts

Cross-team alignment: When multiple teams are working on related projects, share meeting summaries across teams. Instead of each group wondering "What did the other team decide?" They have a searchable record.

Onboarding new team members: New employee joining? Give them access to the past month of meeting transcripts. They can get up to speed on context, decisions, and team dynamics without requiring someone to explain everything.

Pattern recognition: After 20 meetings on the same project, ask your AI tool: "What are the recurring blockers mentioned across these meetings?" or "How has our timeline discussion evolved over these sessions?" You'll spot patterns you'd never catch manually.

Asynchronous participation: Can't attend a meeting? Review the AI summary in 5 minutes instead of asking someone to brief you or watching a 60-minute recording.

4.1.4 What to Watch Out for

The fine print on AI meeting tools varies more than most people realize. Where does the audio go? Who owns it? Can the vendor access it? For routine team meetings, most tools are fine. For anything sensitive, those questions matter a lot more. Know what you're signing up for.

There's also a subtler risk: when people know the AI is capturing everything, some stop paying attention. The transcript becomes a crutch, and the meeting loses the one thing AI can't replicate — people actually thinking together in the room.

Last thing, and maybe the most important: AI is a mirror. It shows you what happened, not what should have happened. A meeting with no clear purpose, no real decisions, no right people in the room — the AI will document all of that faithfully. There's no summary good enough to fix a broken meeting culture. Get that right first, then use AI to make the good stuff even better.

4.2 Language Translation for Global Teams

You manage a team spread across multiple continents. Your developer in Warsaw has a question, your designer in São Paulo has feedback, and your product manager in Tokyo needs clarification. Everyone speaks different levels of English, so nuance can easily get lost and miscommunication can slow progress.

AI translation tools have advanced to the point where they can bridge these gaps in real time, turning language differences from a barrier into barely a bump. Let's look at some tools that make this possible.

4.2.1 Real-Time Translation in Communication Tools

Tool Example #1: Slack's Built-In Translation (Free with Slack)

How it works: When someone posts a message in another language, you can click "Translate" and instantly see it in your language. Powered by AI, it supports dozens of languages.

In an international workplace, employees often feel more confident expressing ideas in their native language. Slack's built-in translation helps preserve clarity while making conversations accessible to everyone.

Tool Example #2: DeepL

Why it stands out: DeepL uses advanced AI to capture nuance, tone, and context more accurately than many traditional translation tools. It is especially effective with European languages.

How to use it:

- Draft emails in your language, translate them with DeepL, and send the translated version
- Upload a PDF and receive a translated version while preserving formatting
- Instantly translate entire web pages or selected text

Manager's Moment

A program manager for a global nonprofit was responsible for overseeing child protection specialists across 16 countries in Asia, Africa, and Central and South America. Each month, he hosted a best-practices meeting where

> country specialists shared what was working, what was changing, and where risks were emerging. Language differences were a huge challenge. Specialists with weak English skills were embarrassed to speak in the meetings, fearing that they would look foolish. Monthly reports came in Spanish, French, Portuguese, Thai, Tagalog, and Indonesian Bahasa, and they required volunteers to translate them into English so that they could be read. By the time all the reports came back from translation, it was already time for the next meeting, and the manager felt unprepared.
>
> The manager began using DeepL to translate the reports into clear, consistent English, saving weeks of waiting and enabling him to identify key issues before each meeting. During the meetings, he encouraged specialists to type their comments in the chat in their native language and used DeepL to quickly translate chats in real time.
>
> The difference was immediate. Instead of surface-level updates, specialists began sharing fuller stories, including patterns of underreporting in one region, innovative community partnerships in another, and early warning signs that might have been overlooked before. The manager began sharing translated summaries of the calls and reports back to each country team, ensuring that insights flowed both ways, not just toward headquarters. By removing the friction of translation, the manager helped the group move from fragmented updates to a shared understanding of how to better protect children while fostering continuous learning across cultures.

AI translation is also transforming virtual meetings by allowing participants to communicate naturally in different languages while still understanding one another in real time.

Tool Example #3: Microsoft® Teams' Live Translation

What it does: During a Teams meeting, turn on live captions in your preferred language. When someone speaks in Japanese, you see captions in English in real-time. This feature supports 40+ languages.

Tool Example #4: Zoom's Live Transcription + Translation (Premium feature)

What it offers: Live captions and translation in multiple languages during video calls. While complex negotiations may still require human interpreters, AI translation works well for standups, project updates, training sessions, and Q&A meetings.

AI translation tools are equally useful for global email and document workflows. Instead of relying entirely on professional translation services, teams can draft content in their preferred language, translate it using tools like DeepL or OpenAI's ChatGPT, and then have a native speaker do a quick review before sharing it globally.

The real power of AI translation goes beyond converting words from one language to another. Modern AI tools can also adapt tone, structure, and communication style to fit cultural expectations. For example, you can ask AI to translate an email into Japanese while also making it more formal and culturally appropriate for Japanese business communication. Instead of producing a literal translation, the AI generates a version with the appropriate greeting structure, tone, and level of formality expected in that context.

4.2.2 Best Practices for AI Translation in Teams

As AI translation becomes more common in daily workflows, the focus should be on using it effectively. The best results come when teams pair AI tools with clear communication practices.

- **Don't rely on AI alone for critical communications.** For legal documents, major announcements, or sensitive HR matters, invest in professional translation. For routine communication, AI is excellent.
- **Teach your team about translation etiquette.** Simple language translates better. Avoid idioms ("hitting it out of the park"), cultural references, or complex metaphors. Write clearly first, then translate.
- **Create translation templates.** For recurring communications (weekly updates, project status reports), create templates that translate well. Test them once with native speakers, then reuse that structure.
- **Build a multilingual glossary.** For company-specific terms, product names, or technical jargon, create a shared glossary showing correct translations. Share this with your team so everyone uses consistent terminology.

When these practices are in place, removing language friction leads to tangible improvements: response times decrease because teams are not waiting on translation, participation increases as people feel comfortable contributing in their own language, misunderstandings reduce due to preserved nuance, and overall team cohesion improves as inclusion becomes more natural. Language diversity then shifts from a challenge to an asset.

4.3 Brainstorming Ideas With AI as a Creative Partner

One of the most valuable things you bring to your team is the ability to ask better questions, explore new perspectives, and solve problems creatively. When used strategically, AI can enhance your creativity by helping you overcome mental blocks, uncover new possibilities, and refine ideas before investing time or resources. One of the most effective ways to do this is through better prompting techniques.

Prompting Technique #1: The Perspective Shift

Instead of asking AI for ideas directly, ask it to think from different perspectives. For example, if your ideas for improving team morale feel repetitive, perspective-based prompting can reveal fresh approaches.

Table 4.1 Example of Perspective-Shift Prompting

Basic prompt	Perspective-shift prompt
Give me ideas to improve team morale.	I need ideas to improve team morale. Generate ideas from these five perspectives: 1. If you were a team member who feels burnt out, what would actually help? 2. If you were an organizational psychologist, what evidence-based approaches would you suggest? 3. If you were a startup founder with a limited budget but high creativity, what would you try? 4. If you were a Fortune 500 CHRO with significant resources, what programs would you implement? 5. If you were a team member in a fully remote setup, what would make the biggest difference? For each perspective, give 2-3 specific, actionable ideas.

Prompting Technique #2: The Constraint Method

Another effective brainstorming strategy is to give AI clear constraints. Limitations force the AI to move beyond generic suggestions and generate ideas that fit your actual situation. For example, imagine your team has just completed a major project, but you have no budget for rewards or gifts. Instead of asking for general recognition ideas, you can define the constraints clearly:

```
- No money to spend
- Remote team (can't do in-person celebration)
- Must feel meaningful
- Should take less than 2 hours to organize
Generate 10 creative recognition ideas that work
within these constraints.
```

This approach prevents generic suggestions ("throw a party," "give bonuses") and forces AI to get creative within your actual limitations.

Prompting Technique #3: The "Yes, And" Technique

A powerful way to collaborate with AI is to use it to expand and refine ideas that are only partially formed. Instead of asking AI to generate something entirely from scratch, you provide the initial concept and ask it to build on it.

For example, you have a rough idea for a new team process but aren't sure how to structure it. Rather than stopping there, you could ask AI to explore the idea further:

```
I have an idea for improving our sprint planning:
instead of one person presenting each ticket, we
could do silent reading first,
then focused discussion.
```

Route Planning

> Build on this idea. What are 5 ways I could structure this to
> maximize effectiveness?
>
> What pitfalls should I avoid? What variations might work even
> better?

AI takes your initial concept and explores variations, identifies risks, and suggests improvements. The process becomes collaborative rather than simply delegating the thinking to AI.

Prompting Technique #4: The Reverse Brainstorm

Sometimes the fastest way to discover better solutions is to ask AI how to create the worst possible outcome.

For example, if you want to improve meeting efficiency, instead of asking AI for better meeting practices, you could ask: "How could I make our team meetings as inefficient, frustrating, and time-wasting as possible?" AI might generate a list of common anti-patterns (e.g., starting late, no agenda, sidebar conversations, unclear decisions, etc).

You can then ask AI to reverse each of those behaviors and turn them into positive practices. By exploring the negative version first, you uncover practical improvements and hidden issues that may not surface through direct brainstorming alone.

Prompting Technique #5: The Scenario Planning Approach

AI can also help you prepare for uncertainty by exploring multiple possible futures instead of planning around a single outcome.

For example, imagine you are planning your team's priorities for the next quarter during an unpredictable market cycle. Instead of creating one fixed plan, you can ask AI to generate optimistic, neutral, and pessimistic scenarios based on factors such as budget changes, hiring capacity, or efficiency pressures. For each scenario, AI can recommend the top priorities to focus on, activities to discontinue, and strategic opportunities worth pursuing.

This approach helps you prepare for multiple possibilities in advance, rather than reacting to uncertainty later.

Remember: Not every AI suggestion will be useful, but even weak ideas can spark new ideas and fresh thinking. That is the real value of AI brainstorming: it helps teams move past creative roadblocks.

Manager's Moment

A Scrum Master for an international nonprofit focused on clean water access was leading sprint planning for the rollout of a new donor management system built on Salesforce. The system would unify how the organization engaged low-, mid-, and major-level donors across regions—but the marketing team, already stretched thin, was hesitant to adopt yet another tool. As she mapped user stories and sprint goals, she realized that adoption was a greater risk than the technical rollout. Instead of relying solely on past experience, she turned to Perplexity AI and prompted: "Help me brainstorm strategies to increase adoption of Salesforce with a resistant marketing team. Include practical tactics, examples, and common pitfalls." Within seconds, she had a strong list of actionable ideas.

With those insights directly built into the sprint plan, she added user stories for creating quick-win dashboards tailored to marketers, built-in short training sessions tied to real campaign work (not generic tutorials), and introduced

> a feedback loop where team members could suggest improvements after each sprint. She also partnered with a respected marketing lead to act as an early adopter and advocate. The resistance softened after a few sprints. The team began to see Salesforce as a tool that actually made their work easier—tracking donor journeys, segmenting communications, and measuring campaign impact more clearly. By using AI to inform her approach, she anticipated the likely resistance and took action to prevent it.

Try This Week

Pick one collaborative challenge to address with AI. Choose the option that addresses your most pressing team challenge right now.

Option 1 - Meetings: In your next team meeting, use Otter.ai or Fireflies.ai to capture notes and action items. Share the AI-generated summary with attendees. Gather feedback on whether it captured everything accurately.

Option 2 - Translation: If you work with non-native English speakers, experiment with DeepL or ChatGPT to translate one email or document into their language. Ask for feedback on quality and whether it made communication easier.

Option 3 - Brainstorming: The next time you're stuck on a problem, spend 15 minutes using one of the creative prompting techniques. See if AI helps you break through the mental block.

When You're Ready

Host an AI brainstorming session with your team and pick a real challenge. Use one of the prompting techniques from this chapter live with your team. Debrief afterward: What worked? What felt forced? How could you use this regularly?

CHAPTER 5

Data-Driven Decision Making

You already have more data than ever before: sales figures, customer feedback, project metrics, employee performance indicators, and budget reports. The challenge is no longer collecting information, but turning it into insights you can act on with confidence.

The good news is that you do not need to be a data scientist to benefit from these tools. You simply need to know which questions to ask and how to interpret the insights AI provides.

5.1 AI-Powered Analytics and Dashboards

Every manager has opened an analytics dashboard full of charts and metrics and wondered, "What am I supposed to do with all this?" The challenge is rarely access to data—it is turning that data into timely, actionable insights.

AI-powered analytics tools help bridge that gap by moving beyond visualization and helping managers interpret what the data actually means.

5.1.1 From Dashboards to Insights: What's Changed

Traditional dashboards mainly report outcomes: sales increased by 12%, website traffic grew, or customer satisfaction scores declined slightly.

AI-powered analytics add context by identifying patterns, explaining likely causes, and highlighting issues that may require attention. For example, instead of only reporting a sales increase, AI can connect that growth to a recent marketing campaign while also flagging slower fulfillment times that could create future operational problems.

In other words, traditional dashboards present information, while AI-powered analytics help turn that information into decisions. Let's look at some tools that make this possible in practice.

5.1.2 Tools That Turn Data into Decisions

Tool Example #1: Microsoft® Power BI with AI features

Microsoft® Power BI's AI uses AI to analyze business data, uncover trends, detect anomalies, and surface insights automatically through dashboards and visual reports.

Key AI features:

- **Smart narratives:** Generates written summaries of dashboard insights
- **Anomaly detection:** Flags unusual spikes or drops in metrics
- **Key influencers:** Shows which factors most impact your target metric
- **Natural language Q&A:** Enables quick insights through conversational search prompts

For readers interested in gaining a deeper understanding of the tool and its practical applications, *Microsoft® Power BI Essentials You Always Wanted to Know* by Dr. Sini V. Pillai provides a clear, step-by-step introduction to building data models and creating interactive dashboards, making it accessible for both technical and non-technical users.

Manager's Moment

A retail operations manager overseeing 64 stores was responsible for making sense of a steady stream of weekly sales data: revenue, foot traffic, conversion rates, and regional performance. Previously, this meant stitching together spreadsheets and scanning for patterns manually, often reacting after issues had already taken root. To get ahead, the manager began using Microsoft® Power BI to centralize and visualize the data. Each week, the system automatically pulled in store-level metrics and generated dashboards that highlighted performance against targets, flagged outliers, and surfaced trends across regions. Instead of combing through rows of numbers, the manager could immediately see which stores were overperforming, which were lagging, and where something unusual was happening.

The real value emerged in the analysis layer. Power® BI helped detect anomalies like a sudden dip in conversion in a high-traffic store or an unexpected spike in returns in a specific region. It pointed to potential drivers such as staffing levels, promotional timing, or inventory gaps. The manager used these insights to guide weekly calls with store leaders, focusing conversations on the few factors that mattered most rather than broad, unfocused reviews. Visualizations made it easier for each store to see their performance in context, creating both accountability and clarity. Over time, the team shifted from reactive problem-solving to proactive management, addressing issues earlier and doubling down on what was working, as data became easier to access and interpret.

Tool Example #2: Salesforce Tableau with CRM Analytics and Einstein AI

Tableau, combined with Salesforce CRM Analytics and Einstein AI, helps organizations analyze data visually, uncover predictive insights, and identify patterns through AI-powered analytics and interactive dashboards. CRM Analytics is Salesforce's native analytics platform integrated within the Salesforce ecosystem.

Key AI features:

- **Einstein Discovery:** Identifies the strongest drivers behind business outcomes
- **Predictive analytics:** Forecasts trends, risks, and future performance
- **Real-time alerts:** Notifies teams when important metrics shift unexpectedly
- **Interactive visualizations:** Makes complex data easier to interpret and explore

Tool Example #3: Google Analytics 4 with AI Insights

Google Analytics 4 (GA4) uses AI to track website and app behavior, identify trends, predict user actions, and recommend optimization opportunities.

Key AI features:

- **Predictive metrics:** Forecasts purchase likelihood and churn risk
- **Automated insights:** Detects meaningful changes in user behavior
- **Behavior analysis:** Identifies actions linked to conversions
- **Cross-platform tracking:** Combines website and app insights in one view

Remember: AI analytics tools are most valuable when paired with human judgment. While AI excels at identifying patterns and correlations, effective decision-making still requires critical thinking and context. When AI suggests "Factor X drives Outcome Y," ask yourself: Is this logical? Could there be a hidden variable? Is this ultimately actionable?

5.1.3 From Insights to Action: A Three-Question Framework

AI analytics can generate valuable insights, but those insights only create value when they lead to informed decisions. To move effectively from insight to action, a simple three-question framework helps determine whether an insight is worth pursuing, testing, or monitoring further. Start by asking:

1. **Is this insight actionable?**
    - If yes: What specific action could I take based on this?
    - If no: Is it still worth monitoring, or is it simply interesting but not useful?
2. **What is the confidence level?**
    - Is this based on strong historical patterns or weak signals?
    - Do I need more data before making a decision?
3. **What is the cost of being wrong?**
    - If the AI insight is incorrect, what is the downside of acting on it?
    - Does the insight justify a small pilot test or a larger commitment?

Example

An AI analytics system identifies the following insight: customers who engage with the support team within the first 30 days show 60% higher retention rates. To evaluate whether this insight should lead to action, the organization applies the three-question framework.

- **Question 1 (Actionable?):** Yes—rather than waiting for customers to reach out, the company could proactively engage new customers early in their journey.
- **Question 2 (Confidence?):** High—the insight is supported by two years of historical data across more than 5,000 customers.
- **Question 3 (Cost of being wrong?):** Low—a proactive outreach campaign is relatively inexpensive and easy to test.

Based on this evaluation, the company decides to launch a pilot program with the next 100 new customers, monitor retention outcomes, and expand the initiative if the results prove successful.

By applying this framework consistently, organizations can avoid both ignoring valuable insights and relying too heavily on unverified AI recommendations.

5.2 Predictive Forecasting for Planning

The future will always involve uncertainty, but AI can help you make educated guesses based on patterns in your historical data. The goal is not to predict the future perfectly. Instead, it is to support better planning and decision-making than relying on intuition alone.

Table 5.1 What AI Forecasting Can Predict (and Can't)

AI excels at:	AI struggles with:
• **Demand patterns:** How many units will we sell next quarter based on historical trends, seasonality, and market conditions?	• **Black swan events:** Pandemics, sudden market crashes, unprecedented disruptions
• **Resource needs:** How many support tickets should we expect next month? How many staff hours will we need?	• **Human decisions:** Your competitor's strategy shifts, regulatory changes, internal reorganizations
• **Project timelines:** Based on our past 50 projects, how long will this new project likely take?	• **Insufficient data:** If you have less than 6-12 months of historical data, predictions become less reliable
• **Customer behavior:** Which customers are most likely to churn in the next 90 days? Which leads are most likely to convert?	
• **Budget requirements:** What will our operational costs likely be next quarter?	

The key is to use AI forecasting for the more predictable aspects of business operations while remaining adaptable to unexpected changes and uncertainty.

5.2.1 Tools for Predictive Forecasting

Tool Example #1: Adaptive Insights (Workday Adaptive Planning)

Workday Adaptive Planning uses AI-powered forecasting to help organizations predict future revenue, expenses, cash flow, workforce needs, and operational performance using historical and real-time business data.

Key AI features:

- **Scenario modeling:** Tests "what-if" situations and projects financial outcomes
- **Predictive forecasting:** Estimates future revenue, costs, and business trends
- **Automated reporting:** Generates real-time planning and performance insights
- **Collaborative planning:** Aligns finance, operations, and workforce forecasting in one platform

Tool Example #2: Google Sheets with Built-in Forecasting (Free option)

Google Sheets includes built-in forecasting functions that use historical data and statistical models to predict future values, making it a simple and accessible option for basic forecasting tasks.

Key AI features:

- **Trend analysis:** Identifies patterns across sales, demand, or operational data
- **Automated calculations:** Instantly generates projections from existing datasets
- **Google AI integration:** Supports more advanced predictive modeling through Google's AI and machine learning tools

How to use it:

- Set up your historical data in columns (dates and values)
- Use =FORECAST.LINEAR(future_date, known_values, known_dates)
- Google Sheets calculates the projected value

5.2.2 Making Forecasting Actionable

Once forecasting tools are in place, the next step is understanding how to apply them in real business situations. A structured workflow helps organizations move from raw historical data to actionable planning decisions.

Step 1: Gather historical data

Begin by collecting relevant historical information. For example, a customer support team may analyze the past two years of monthly ticket volume while also identifying seasonal trends, such as post-holiday spikes in January.

Step 2: Use AI to forecast

Next, use an analytics platform or AI assistant to analyze historical trends and generate future projections. A prompt might look like this:

> I have customer support ticket data for the past 24 months:
>
> [Paste your monthly data]
>
> Analyze this for:
>
> **1.** Overall trend (increasing/decreasing/stable)
>
> **2.** Seasonal patterns
>
> **3.** Forecast ticket volume for next 3 months
>
> **4.** Show confidence intervals (best case, likely case, worst case)

Step 3: Interpret the results

AI might show: "Based on historical patterns, expect 3,200-3,800 tickets next quarter (likely: 3,500). This represents a 12% increase over the same quarter last year."

Step 4: Plan with flexibility

Use the forecast to plan staffing needs while allowing room for unexpected increases in demand. In this example, staffing may be optimized for approximately 3,500 tickets while maintaining enough flexibility to handle a possible increase to 3,800.

> **Manager's Moment**
>
> A sales director overseeing three regions of a national restaurant chain reviewed the forecasts from his site managers and noticed that every region projected growth, despite clear challenges. Rather than relying on instinct alone, he used Einstein (Salesforce's AI) to perform a scenario-based analysis. He prompted it with two likely constraints: ongoing seafood supply disruptions due to a long-haul trucking strike, and persistent waitstaff shortages. Asking Einstein to use historical data and these constraints, he asked it to estimate how limited seafood availability would reduce menu variety and average ticket size in his regions and how staffing gaps would cap table turns and slow service across all regions. The adjusted projections told a different story: even strong locations would likely miss targets if these constraints persisted, not because of demand, but because of capacity.
>
> Armed with this clearer picture, he shifted his coaching approach. Instead of asking managers to "be more realistic," he asked them to build forecasts around constraints and showed them how to use Einstein to create stronger projections. He introduced a simple framework: input key assumptions (i.e., staffing levels, supply reliability), model scenarios for best-case, expected, and constrained situations, and tie projections to operational capacity—not just demand. Over time, managers began submitting forecasts that included assumptions, risks, and

> contingencies. The tone changed from optimism-driven projections to evidence-based planning, enabling the organization to set achievable targets and make smarter decisions about staffing, sourcing, and promotions.

5.2.3 Best Practices for Forecasting

- **Use multiple scenarios.** Don't just forecast the most likely outcome. Create three scenarios: optimistic, realistic, pessimistic. Plan for the realistic, but prepare for the pessimistic.
- **Update forecasts regularly.** A forecast made in January using data through December is already outdated by March. Re-run predictions as new data comes in.
- **Combine AI with human judgment.** AI forecasts based on patterns. You know about upcoming changes AI can't see (new product launch, major client win, team reorganization). Adjust AI forecasts with your insider knowledge.
- **Track forecast accuracy.** After the quarter ends, compare AI predictions to actual results. If AI consistently over-predicts or under-predicts, you can adjust future forecasts accordingly.
- **Communicate uncertainty.** When sharing forecasts with stakeholders, always include confidence ranges. "We forecast 3,500 tickets, but it could range from 3,200 to 3,800" is more honest and useful than "We forecast 3,500" presented as certainty.

5.3 Risk Assessment Tools

Every decision carries risk. The challenge is identifying those risks before they become major problems. AI risk assessment tools analyze patterns across data to detect financial,

Route Planning

operational, project, and security risks—often earlier than human observation alone.

By continuously monitoring trends and anomalies, these tools help organizations shift from reactive responses to proactive risk management. The following examples show how AI supports risk assessment across different business areas.

5.3.1 Project Risk Assessment

Projects often fail due to early warning signs like delayed tasks, overloaded resources, or missing ownership. However, these warning signs are easy to miss when teams are managing multiple priorities simultaneously. Tools like Microsoft® Project with AI insights or Monday.com use AI to analyze task progress, workload, and dependencies to flag at-risk projects early.

Example alerts:

- "Only 40% of tasks completed on time → HIGH risk of delay"
- "Resource overallocated at 120% → MEDIUM risk of burnout"
- "Critical tasks unassigned → HIGH risk of stall"

5.3.2 Financial Risk Monitoring

Financial risks are often detected too late in monthly or quarterly reports. By then, the opportunity to correct the issue early may already be lost. Platforms such as Ramp and Oracle NetSuite monitor real-time spending and flag anomalies.

Example alerts:

- "Software subscription spending increased 35% this month → unusual compared to 6-month average"
- "Monthly budget overrun pattern in Department X"

- "Three vendors increased prices this quarter → projected annual impact: $47K"

Manager's Moment

A people analytics manager supporting a national organization was asked to anticipate workforce risks across several markets where hiring demand was rising quickly. Instead of relying on lagging indicators, the manager turned to Workday's predictive analytics to examine patterns in staff acquisition, onboarding, and retention. By analyzing metrics like time-to-fill (speed to hire), time-to-productivity (speed to full proficiency), early turnover rates, and candidate pipeline strength, the system revealed risk signals by region. In one market, extended hiring cycles combined with high competition for talent suggested future staffing gaps. In another, hires were coming in quickly but taking significantly longer to reach full proficiency, pointing to onboarding or training weaknesses that could impact performance and morale.

Using these insights, the manager partnered with HR and local leaders to take targeted action. In slower hiring markets, they adjusted sourcing strategies and streamlined interview processes to reduce delays. In regions with slower ramp-up times, they redesigned onboarding by adding structured training milestones, mentorship, and clearer role expectations. The manager also flagged markets with higher early attrition risk, prompting proactive engagement efforts during the first 90 days. Over time, hiring became more predictable, new employees reached effectiveness faster, and retention stabilized. By using predictive analytics, the organization moved from reacting to workforce challenges to anticipating them.

5.3.3 Customer Churn Risk Assessment

Customers often show silent signs of dissatisfaction before leaving. If you could predict which customers are at risk of leaving, you could intervene before they churn. Customer success platforms like Gainsight, ChurnZero, or Vitally use AI to score churn risk based on engagement patterns, support ticket history, usage trends, and payment behavior.

Risk factors AI monitors:

- Declining product usage or reduced login frequency
- Increased support tickets with negative sentiment
- Key stakeholder turnover at the customer's company
- Lack of engagement with new features
- Payment delays or disputes

AI helps organizations identify behavioral warning signs early, enabling customer success teams to strengthen relationships and improve retention outcomes.

5.3.4 Security and Compliance Risk

Security breaches and compliance failures often emerge from subtle behavioral changes or system irregularities that are difficult to detect consistently. Platforms like Darktrace (cybersecurity) or Drata (compliance monitoring) use AI to establish baseline "normal" behavior and flag deviations.

Example alerts:

- "User account logged in from two different countries within 30 minutes—possible credential compromise"
- "Unusual bulk data access detected"
- "Unauthorized configuration change"

AI-powered risk monitoring helps organizations move from reactive problem-solving to proactive prevention. When used effectively, these tools support faster interventions, reduced losses, and more stable operations by turning hidden risks into actionable signals.

5.3.5 Making Risk Assessment Actionable

AI-based risk detection is only valuable when it leads to timely action. To ensure risks are handled effectively, a simple workflow can be used to move from alert to resolution in a structured way.

Table 5.2 Risk Assessment Response Workflow With Customer Churn Example

Response Workflow	Example
Alert triggers: AI flags a potential risk	AI flags Customer ABC as high churn risk due to a 60% drop in engagement
Quick validation: Confirm whether it is a real issue or a false positive	Check if the drop aligns with seasonal or business cycle patterns
Assign ownership: Allocate responsibility for investigation or resolution	Customer success manager takes ownership
Action plan: Define and execute corrective steps	Schedule a check-in call, review goals, and identify blockers
Follow-up: Track whether the intervention worked	Monitor engagement over the next 30 days
Learn: Capture insights to improve future risk detection and response	Document outcomes and refine the churn prediction model

This approach enables organizations to detect risks early, respond in a structured way, and continuously improve their decision-making, reducing the likelihood of issues escalating into major disruptions.

Try This Week

Pick one data-driven decision you're facing right now:

Option 1 - Analytics: Identify one decision you need to make this month. Use an AI analytics tool (Power BI, Tableau, or even ChatGPT with your data) to surface insights that inform that decision.

Option 2 - Forecasting: Take historical data from one area of your business (sales, support tickets, project timelines) and use AI to forecast the next quarter. Compare the AI forecast to your gut instinct. Track which was more accurate.

Option 3 - Risk Assessment: Review your current projects or customer base. Use AI to identify top 3 risks. For each, create a simple mitigation plan.

When You're Ready

- **Build a "Decision Dashboard":** Identify the 5 most important recurring decisions you make (budget allocation, hiring, project prioritization, etc.). For each, define: What data would help me decide better? What AI tool could provide that data? Consolidate these insights into a simple dashboard so key information is available at the point of decision-making.
- **Establish a risk review ritual:** Block 30 minutes weekly to review AI-generated risk alerts. Don't just react; look for patterns. Are certain types of risks recurring? Can you put preventive measures in place?

PART 3

Managing AI Adoption in Your Team

At this stage, you've already experienced AI's value firsthand—you've saved time, improved decisions, and seen what it can do in practice. Now the focus shifts from individual use to something more challenging and more important: helping your team experience those same benefits.

This is where your role expands. You're no longer just using AI—you're helping others adopt it in a way that feels natural, safe, and useful, without the resistance or overwhelm that often comes with new technology.

In GPS terms, this is active navigation. The system is no longer just helping you choose a direction; it is guiding you in real time: "In 500 feet, turn right." Part 3 works the same way, supporting you as you move from personal use to team-wide adoption.

It helps you:

- Bring your team along gradually without overwhelming them
- Set clear guardrails around ethics, privacy, and trust
- Respond effectively when implementation doesn't go as planned

Remember, successful AI adoption rarely happens all at once. Teams that get it right start small, build confidence through early wins, and expand step by step.

Now the journey is no longer just about knowing the route—it is about guiding others through it with you.

CHAPTER 6

Introducing AI Without Overwhelming People

At the team adoption stage, many AI initiatives fall short—not because the tools don't work, but because the human side of change is overlooked. Teams are pushed toward adoption without context, overwhelmed with new workflows, or asked to trust systems they haven't been guided through.

This chapter offers a practical roadmap for introducing AI in a way that builds understanding, reduces resistance, and supports steady, sustainable adoption across your team.

6.1 Communicating the Benefits Clearly

The way you introduce AI to your team will determine whether they see it as an opportunity or a threat. Your communication strategy matters more than the specific tools you choose.

6.1.1 Why Most AI Introductions Fail

The biggest barriers are often communication-related, and many initiatives fail because of avoidable messaging mistakes such as:

Mistake #1: Leading with technology instead of problems

✗ "We're rolling out this new AI tool called [Tool Name]. Here's how it works..."

✅ "Remember how we all hate spending hours in meetings summarizing what we discussed? I found a way to eliminate that."

Mistake #2: Vague benefits instead of concrete wins

❌ "AI will make us more efficient and productive."

✅ "This tool will save each of you approximately 3-5 hours per week on email management and meeting notes."

Mistake #3: Ignoring fears instead of addressing them

❌ Avoiding conversations about job security concerns

✅ "I know some of you might be worried AI will replace your role. Let me be direct about what will and won't change..."

Mistake #4: Top-down mandate instead of invitation

❌ "Starting Monday, everyone must use this AI tool."

✅ "I've been testing this AI tool and it's been incredibly helpful. I'd love a few volunteers to pilot it with me and share feedback."

When leaders focus on real problems, clear benefits, honest concerns, and inclusive rollout strategies, AI is far more likely to be seen as a helpful support system rather than a forced change.

6.1.2 The Three-Part Communication Framework

When introducing AI to your team, structure your communication around three elements:

Problem → Solution → Safety.

Part 1: Problem (What Pain Are We Solving?)

Start with a real, familiar frustration your team already experiences. This approach validates existing issues, making the need for change immediately relatable.

> **Example**
>
> "I've noticed we're all drowning in meeting notes. Last month alone, our team had 47 meetings. That's roughly 8-10 hours per person just in meetings, plus another 2-3 hours writing up notes and action items afterward. That's time we could be spending on actual work instead of documenting work."

Part 2: Solution (How AI Addresses This Specific Problem)

Introduce AI as a focused fix for that specific problem, not as a broad transformation.

> **Example**
>
> "I've been testing an AI tool that automatically transcribes our meetings, generates summaries, and extracts action items. It's like having a dedicated note-taker in every meeting. What used to take me 20-30 minutes after each meeting now takes 2 minutes of quick review."

Part 3: Safety (Addressing Fears Directly)

Address potential fears before they become objections.

> **Example**
>
> "I want to address a few things upfront:
>
> **Job security:** This tool doesn't replace anyone on our team. It handles admin work so you can focus on the strategic and creative parts of your job that AI can't do.

Privacy: Meeting transcripts are only accessible to our team. Nothing leaves our workspace. You can always turn it off for sensitive discussions.

Ease of use: You don't need to learn anything new. The tool works in the background. I'll show you the basics in 5 minutes.

Adoption: This is optional for the first month. I'm inviting volunteers to try it. If it works well, we'll expand. If it doesn't, we'll adjust or find something else."

Manager's Moment

An IT director at a mid-sized organization was tasked with introducing AI for the first time, an initiative that drew both curiosity and skepticism. Rather than launching a broad, abstract "AI transformation," she started with a narrow, practical entry point: research and internal knowledge work. She introduced Perplexity AI as a pilot tool, positioning it not as a replacement for expertise but as a faster way to find, summarize, and validate information with cited sources. Her rollout strategy was intentionally lightweight. She identified a small group of early adopters across departments, gave them three specific use cases (summarizing industry trends, answering internal policy questions, and preparing meeting briefings), and provided simple, copy-and-paste prompts to lower the barrier to entry. Within days, those users were saving time and sharing examples with peers.

To accelerate adoption, she focused on visibility and momentum rather than mandates. She asked early adopters to demonstrate one real use case in team meetings, showing how a five-minute query replaced a 30-minute search, and created a shared space where employees could post "before and after" examples of their work. She also established clear guardrails to ensure AI was used responsibly and in alignment with company values, clarifying when employees should verify outputs, how to manage sensitive information, and which decisions still required human judgment. As confidence grew, usage spread organically. Through small actions of encouragement and visible value, the IT director helped her company embrace AI in daily work.

Bonus Online Resources

Access the online resources for a set of ready-to-use communication templates to support AI adoption. These include formats for announcing pilot programs, introducing AI in team meetings, and handling one-on-one conversations with hesitant team members.

6.2 Training Options for Non-Technical Staff

Once people agree to try AI, the next barrier is: "I don't know how to use this." The way you train your team will determine whether adoption feels natural or overwhelming.

The good news is that most modern AI tools are designed for non-technical users. So, the real barrier is not complexity, but intimidation. Your goal is to make learning simple, practical, and immediately useful. To do this effectively, you can use one or more of the following approaches:

Introduce One Use Case at a Time

The most common training mistake is trying to cover everything in one go. Long, feature-heavy sessions feel thorough, but they tend to produce the opposite of the intended effect. Employees become overwhelmed, tell themselves they'll "revisit the training later," and never quite get started. A far more effective approach is to pick a single high-value use case and let people experience its benefit right away.

Start with something concrete and low-stakes, like AI meeting notes. In a 15-minute session, show how the tool captures a discussion, surfaces key points, and pulls out action items. That's it. Once people see it working in their own context, curiosity takes over. You can introduce the next use case when the first one has settled and each addition feels like progress rather than pressure.

Train People for Their Actual Role

A team lead, an executive, and an individual contributor do not approach AI from the same place. When learning paths are tailored to roles, training feels more relevant and when it feels relevant, people are far more likely to apply it in practice.

For *individual contributors,* the focus should be personal productivity: drafting emails faster, processing information more efficiently, handling the repetitive parts of their role. Short 15-minute demos work well, especially when followed immediately by a "try it yourself" exercise. Weekly drop-in office hours also give people a low-pressure space to ask questions as they arise.

For *team leads* and *project managers,* the more compelling entry point is coordination: using AI to handle meeting outputs, streamline status reporting, and improve decision-making through better information. Thirty-minute sessions grounded in real project scenarios tend to resonate more strongly. Monthly peer sessions then help maintain momentum as leads share what's working in practice.

For *senior leaders,* the value proposition is synthesis and speed, and AI becomes a natural fit for both. Executives respond well to an executive briefing format that leads with ROI and uses AI for board summaries, competitive intelligence, and scenario stress-testing. Don't train executives like everyone else. Give them short, high-value briefings and personalized support instead of group sessions.

Let Peers Carry the Learning Forward

No matter how well you design the training, you can't be everywhere at once. The most durable adoption happens when the knowledge lives inside the team, not just with the manager.

This is where internal champions become critical. A small group—usually two or three people who are naturally curious about new tools—can be trained more deeply, given better resources, and empowered to support others through weekly office hours. People often learn more freely from peers than from managers, asking better questions and experimenting more openly in that environment.

Recruitment can be as simple as: "I'm looking for a few people who want to go deeper on AI and help the team get comfortable with it—anyone interested?" In most cases, someone will volunteer immediately. The next step is to invest in them visibly, through time, access, and recognition. Once the team sees that champions are valued, the momentum of AI adoption begins to sustain itself.

Key Communication Principles to Remember

- **Be specific rather than general.** "Save time" is vague, but "reduce time spent on weekly reports from 2 hours to 30 minutes" is clear and actionable.
- **Show, don't just tell.** A short 2-minute demo often communicates more than a long explanation.

- **Acknowledge limitations.** No technology is perfect, and being transparent about constraints builds trust.
- **Use team language, not vendor language.** Avoid repeating marketing terms from AI tools, instead, translate features into benefits your team actually understands and values.
- **Make it opt-in initially.** Early volunteers become natural champions, while mandates tend to create resistance.

6.3 Starting Small: Low-Risk Project Ideas

The biggest mistake in AI adoption is trying to do too much, too fast. When you start with complex, high-stakes use cases, tools often buckle under the pressure, teams get overwhelmed, and everyone walks away convinced that AI simply doesn't work. The smarter path is the opposite: start with something small, where success is easy to measure, failure costs little, and the learning curve is short enough that employees feel encouraged to continue.

The four pilots in this section are built around exactly that principle. Each one targets a real, recognizable pain point, can be implemented within a week, and delivers results that are visible enough to build momentum for broader adoption.

Pilot 1: AI-Powered Meeting Notes

Most teams spend somewhere between 30-60 minutes per meeting just capturing what was said—writing notes, chasing action items, formatting summaries. It's a high-frequency administrative task that AI can streamline almost immediately. Tools like Otter.ai or Fireflies.ai transcribe the conversation, generate a summary, and pull out action items in the time it takes to grab a coffee after the call.

Table 6.1 4-Week AI Meeting Pilot Plan

Week	Focus	What to do
1	Leadership pilot	Run the tool in one recurring meeting. Spend 10 minutes reviewing the output together by analyzing what it captured or what it missed.
2	Volunteer expansion	Invite 2–3 teams to try it. Share a 5-minute setup guide and check in mid-week.
3	Refine	Gather feedback. Identify which meeting formats work best and adjust accordingly.
4	Decide	If satisfaction is 75%+, expand. If mixed, refine the scope before proceeding further.

The aim is to deliver clear efficiency improvements with minimal disruption to existing workflows, while building enough confidence and value that most participants continue using the tool beyond the pilot.

Pilot 2: AI Email Assistant for Customer Support

Customer support teams often spend the majority of their day writing variations of the same email. The questions change slightly, the tone shifts a little, but the underlying response—the policy, the process, the next step—stays largely the same. That pattern is exactly what AI handles well. The idea isn't to remove humans from the process. It's to let AI handle the difficult first draft so people can spend their time editing, personalizing, and improving the message instead of staring at a blank page.

Table 6.2 4-Week AI Customer Support Pilot Plan

Week	Focus	What to do
1	Build the template library	Identify the 10 most common inquiries. Work with 1–2 support staff to write AI prompts for each—specify the tone, required information, and length. Save the best versions in a shared document.
2	Train the team	Run a 15-minute session showing how to pull up a template, customize it for a specific customer, and send something that feels personal. Establish the rule early: AI drafts, humans approve.
3	Expand	Survey the team on time savings and quality. Fill gaps in the template library based on what they're actually encountering.
4	Evaluate	Use response time and customer satisfaction scores to decide how broadly to roll this out.

The goal is to create noticeable improvements in response speed while maintaining service quality, without compromising customer satisfaction.

Pilot 3: AI Document Summarization for Leadership

Senior leaders are often expected to review 20–30 page reports before important meetings. In reality, many do not fully read them—not due to lack of interest, but because time is limited. AI can help close that gap by quickly turning lengthy documents into concise, decision-focused summaries. The process is simple: feed a document into Claude or ChatGPT with a prompt that asks for key achievements, risks, and decisions needed — all in under 500 words.

Table 6.3 4-Week AI Document Summarization Pilot Plan

Week	Focus	What to do
1	Calibrate	Test with one recurring report. Compare the AI summary to what you'd write by hand. Refine the prompt until the quality is consistently trustworthy.
2	Leadership pilot	Before the next leadership meeting, summarize all pre-read materials. Send both versions—original and summary. Ask at the meeting who used which, and whether summaries were sufficient.
3	Systematize	Create standard prompts for different document types. Assign ownership for running documents through AI. Set a quality check before anything gets distributed.
4	Measure	Track pre-read time saved and meeting preparedness. Identify where else this pattern applies.

The objective is to significantly reduce the time leaders spend reviewing materials before meetings while ensuring AI-generated summaries are accurate and useful enough for decision-making. Better preparation leads to higher-quality discussions, faster alignment, and more productive meetings overall.

Pilot 4: AI-Assisted Content Creation for Marketing

Marketing teams are under constant pressure to produce more content across more channels—social posts, blog outlines, email campaigns, ad copy—often without any increase in team size. AI is unlikely to replace the creative judgment that makes content engaging and effective, but it can dramatically reduce one of the most exhausting parts of the process: starting from a blank page.

Table 6.4 4-Week AI Content Creation Pilot Plan

Week	Focus	What to do
1	Find what works	Have one person generate content using AI, iterating on prompts until the output is consistently usable. The goal isn't volume—it's identifying the prompt patterns that match your brand's tone.
2	Expand the team	Bring in 2–3 more team members. Share the prompts that performed well and build a shared library. Daily check-ins help surface small improvements quickly.
3	Add content formats	Apply the same workflow to blog outlines, email subject lines, and ad copy. The rule stays the same across all of them: nothing goes out without review.
4	Evaluate honestly	Assess which content types genuinely benefited from AI, which still need to be fully human, and what the engagement data actually shows.

The goal is to increase content output by 40–60% while keeping engagement metrics stable or trending upward. For many marketing teams, that level of scalability can unlock opportunities that previously felt constrained by time and bandwidth.

Manager's Moment

A call center manager at a government watchdog organization was struggling to keep customer service agents up to date. Callers frequently asked about legislative changes, policy updates, and breaking developments faster than the organization's internal knowledge base could realistically keep pace. To close the gap, the manager introduced Guru, enhanced with its AI-powered search and content suggestions. Instead of requiring agents to dig

through static documents, Guru delivered the most relevant, verified answers in real time, even as topics evolved.
To build support, the manager invited a pilot group of respected agents to test the tool during live calls, contribute improvements to answers, and shape how information was organized. When those agents began sharing how quickly they could find accurate, up-to-date responses, especially on fast-moving legislative issues, skepticism across the team began to ease.

As adoption grew, the manager reinforced a simple rhythm: trust, but verify. Content in Guru was regularly reviewed by policy experts, and agents could flag gaps or outdated information with one click. During calls, agents used the tool to quickly pull summaries of new bills, clarify organizational positions, or explain how recent legislative changes affected constituents. It also helped them respond to questions tied to current events—surfacing context, timelines, and approved messaging without requiring agents to become policy experts overnight. Over time, call handling became faster and more consistent, and agents reported greater confidence in navigating complex conversations. By involving agents early and making the tool visibly useful, the manager turned knowledge management from a bottleneck into a shared, living resource.

Try This Week

Choose one small pilot project from this chapter:

Map it to your team's biggest current frustration. Use the step-by-step guide to plan Week 1. Don't launch yet—just plan. Share your plan with one trusted team member and get their input.

Alternative: If you're not ready for a full pilot, start with communication. Draft an email or meeting script using one of the templates in this chapter. Send it or schedule the meeting for next week.

When You're Ready

Create your 4-week pilot roadmap:

- Week 1: What's the test?
- Week 2: Who's involved?
- Week 3: How do we measure success?
- Week 4: What's the decision criteria to expand, refine, or stop?

Identify your champions:

Who on your team is naturally curious about AI? Have a conversation with them about becoming peer trainers. You don't need a formal program yet—just begin creating internal advocates.

CHAPTER 7

AI Ethics and Trust

As AI becomes more integrated into everyday work, the conversation can no longer focus only on productivity and efficiency. Managers also need to consider how AI affects fairness, privacy, accountability, and trust across the organization.

This chapter examines three essential areas of responsible AI use: minimizing bias, protecting privacy and security, and establishing clear policies that guide decision-making. These foundations are what turn AI from a short-term productivity tool into a sustainable and trusted part of the workplace.

7.1 Avoiding Bias in AI Tools

AI systems learn from historical data. If that data contains biased patterns, AI can unintentionally reproduce and amplify them.

This is not because AI is intentionally discriminatory, but because it reflects the patterns present in past decisions and behaviors. As a manager, your role is to recognize where bias may appear and ensure important decisions still involve human oversight.

7.1.1 How Bias Shows Up in AI

- **Hiring and recruitment:** An AI resume-screening system trained on past hiring decisions may begin favoring candidates who resemble previously hired employees.

For example, if a company's engineering team has historically been predominantly male, the system may unintentionally downrank qualified female candidates because it associates past hiring patterns with "successful" applicants.

- **Performance evaluation:** AI tools analyzing productivity or performance data may unintentionally penalize employees who take parental leave, work flexible schedules, or have employment gaps—patterns that can disproportionately affect caregivers and underrepresented groups.
- **Customer service:** AI chatbots trained on historical interactions may provide inconsistent service quality based on names, language patterns, or geographic indicators, unintentionally disadvantaging certain customer groups.
- **Credit and lending:** AI systems assessing financial risk may rely on indirect indicators, such as zip codes, that correlate with protected characteristics like race or income level, potentially reinforcing historical discrimination patterns.
- **Resource allocation:** AI tools recommending promotions, training opportunities, or leadership development programs may favor employees who resemble historically promoted groups, limiting opportunities for underrepresented employees.

If managers are not actively monitoring outcomes, AI can easily perpetuate such historical inequalities.

7.1.2 How to Detect and Prevent Bias

Test for disparate impact. Before deploying any AI tool that affects people (hiring, promotions, performance reviews, customer treatment), analyze whether outcomes differ across demographic groups. Ask:

- Does the tool consistently favor certain groups over others?
- Are recommendation or approval rates relatively balanced?
- Can any disparities be explained by legitimate, non-discriminatory factors?

For example, if an AI resume-screening tool advances 40% of male applicants but only 15% of female applicants, that signals a potential bias issue that needs investigation.

Diversify your training data. If you're building custom AI models/templates or fine-tuning existing ones, ensure your training data represents the diversity of people affected by the AI's decisions.

Keep humans involved in high-stakes decisions. AI should support decisions, not make them independently. Hiring, firing, promotions, and disciplinary actions still require human judgment and accountability.

Review outcomes regularly. Bias checks should be ongoing, not one-time audits. Regularly review AI-assisted decisions, look for uneven patterns across groups, and pay attention to concerns raised by employees or customers.

Manager's Moment

A talent acquisition manager at a national services firm began noticing a pattern in candidates filtered out by HireVue. The system was consistently downgrading applicants with gaps in their employment history, flagging them as higher risk or lower fit. At first glance, the logic seemed reasonable, but a deeper review revealed unintended bias. Many of the rejected candidates had taken time off for caregiving, military service transitions, health recovery, or further education. These were not indicators of poor performance, yet the AI had learned to treat them as negative signals based on historical hiring data. As a result, the organization was quietly excluding capable, diverse candidates, especially women re-entering the workforce and individuals from non-linear career paths.

Rather than abandoning the tool, the manager worked with HR, legal, and data teams to address the bias directly. They audited the screening criteria, retrained the model to avoid penalizing employment gaps automatically, and adopted a more holistic evaluation of candidate experience. They introduced human review checkpoints for flagged applicants and added structured questions to better understand the context behind career breaks. The manager also revised hiring guidelines and trained recruiters and hiring managers to better value non-traditional career paths. Over time, the candidate pool became more diverse, and several hires who would previously have been filtered out proved to be strong performers.

7.1.3 When You Can't Fully Eliminate Bias

Sometimes you can't remove bias completely, especially with third-party AI tools where you don't control the training data or algorithm. In those cases:

- **Acknowledge limitations openly.** Tell your team: "This tool isn't perfect. It may have biases we can't fully eliminate. That's why human review is mandatory."
- **Layer multiple inputs.** Don't rely on AI alone. Combine AI recommendations with human interviews, diverse panel reviews, structured assessments, and other methods to balance out AI's blind spots.

- **Monitor continuously.** Even when the AI system itself cannot be changed, you can still detect concerning patterns in outcomes and take corrective action. Track metrics, investigate anomalies, and question recommendations that seem inconsistent or unreasonable.
- **Consider not using AI at all.** If a tool consistently produces biased outcomes and you can't mitigate them, stop using it. No efficiency gain is worth systemic discrimination.

7.1.4 Building a Bias-Aware Culture

Beyond technical fixes, create a team culture where people feel comfortable to flag potential bias. You can support this by:

- **Normalizing questions about AI.** Encourage your team to ask: "Why did the AI recommend this? Does this outcome make sense? Are we seeing any patterns that concern us?"
- **Creating clear reporting channels.** Make it easy for employees, customers, or stakeholders to report suspected bias without fear of retaliation.
- **Training teams on bias awareness.** Help employees understand how bias appears in AI systems and why human oversight matters. Even brief training sessions can significantly improve a team's ability to identify problems early.

Avoiding bias is not about achieving perfection. It is about maintaining vigilance, transparency, and a consistent commitment to fairness.

7.2 Privacy and Data Security Considerations

AI tools rely heavily on data, and that data often includes sensitive information such as customer details, employee records, financial information, internal communications, or proprietary business data.

Every time you feed data into an AI tool, you're making a decision about privacy and security. One wrong call can lead to data breaches, regulatory violations, loss of customer trust, and legal liability.

7.2.1 Understand Where Your Data Goes

Not all AI tools handle data the same way. Before adopting any AI platform, understand how it stores, accesses, and uses your organization's information by asking questions such as:

- **Where is the data stored?**
  Is it stored on cloud servers, local devices, or a hybrid system? If cloud-based, where are those servers located?
- **Who can access the data?**
  Is access limited to your organization, or can vendors, employees, or subcontractors also view it?
- **Is the data used for AI training?**
  Will your inputs help improve the model for other users, and can you opt out of that process?
- **How long is data retained?**
  Does the vendor delete information after processing, and can deletion requests be made?
- **What happens if there is a breach?**
  What security measures, notification policies, and liability protections are in place?

AI convenience should never come at the expense of privacy or security. Managers must be thoughtful about what data is shared, how it is protected, and where clear boundaries are needed. Figure 7.1 shows a simple framework for deciding what data should and should not be shared.

Figure 7.1 **The Data Sharing Hierarchy for AI Tools**

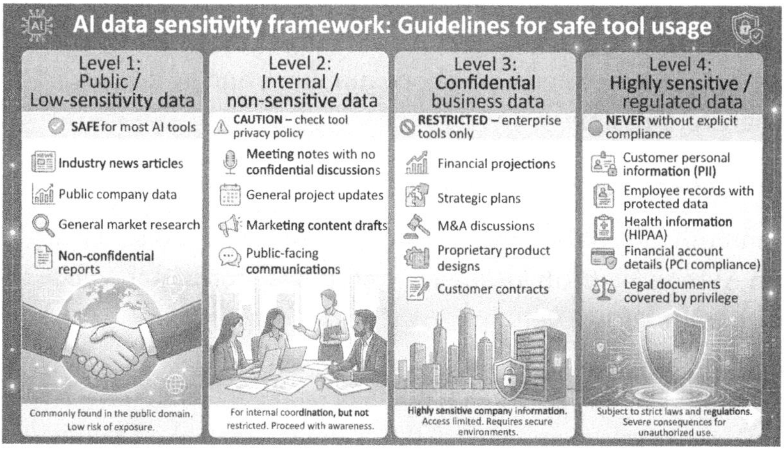

AI Tool: Google Gemini

Prompt: Generate a visual illustrating a framework for deciding what data could be shared.

7.2.2 Practical Privacy Protection Strategies

Effective privacy protection is less about restricting AI use and more about creating clear boundaries for what data is safe to use and how it should be handled. In practice, this comes down to a few simple but important safeguards:

Use Enterprise Versions of AI Tools

Free AI tools often come with limited privacy guarantees. Enterprise versions typically provide stronger protections, including data processing agreements (DPAs), commitments not to use your data for model training, and enhanced security and compliance certifications (such as SOC 2, GDPR, or HIPAA, where applicable). While enterprise plans may cost more per user, they significantly reduce exposure to costly data breaches or compliance violations.

Anonymize Before Processing

Before sharing information with AI tools, remove or replace personally identifiable information. For example, use placeholders like "Customer A" or "Employee 1," and strip out details such as emails, phone numbers, and addresses wherever possible.

Keep Sensitive Data in Controlled Environments

Don't upload confidential files to web-based AI tools. Instead, use AI tools that run locally on your devices or within your company's secure network.

Train Your Team on Data Classification

Create a simple framework: "If this data were leaked publicly, what would happen?" If the answer is "lawsuit," "competitive disadvantage," or "regulatory violation," the data should not be used in AI tools without proper safeguards.

> **Manager's Moment**
>
> A pharmacy manager, serving multiple assisted living facilities, noticed unusually fast turnaround times from one technician reviewing complex medication profiles. Upon investigation, she found that the technician had been copying patient medication lists into ChatGPT to quickly check for drug interactions. While well-intentioned, this raised serious concerns around patient privacy, regulatory compliance, and the safety of relying on AI outputs without proper clinical oversight.

> The manager addressed it constructively rather than punitively, using it as a team-wide learning opportunity. She reinforced strict data privacy rules prohibiting the use of external AI tools with protected health information and partnered with IT to explore compliant, healthcare-grade alternatives. She also introduced clear guidelines on where AI could be safely used, such as general education or workflow support without patient data. The technician was included in evaluating safer tools. Over time, the team improved both efficiency and compliance, reinforcing that innovation and responsibility must go hand in hand, especially where patient trust is at stake.

7.2.3 Building a Privacy-First Culture

Privacy and security are not barriers to AI adoption; they are guardrails that enable it to scale safely and sustainably. Privacy must be treated as everyone's responsibility, not just IT's. Teams should be regularly reminded of the following:

- "Before using an AI tool, think about what data you're sharing."
- "When in doubt, ask—checking is better than creating a breach."
- "If a tool requests sensitive data, pause and escalate before proceeding."

Organizations should also introduce a simple approval process for new AI tools. This ensures that no tool is adopted without basic safeguards in place, including security and compliance review, manager approval, and IT validation for anything that touches company data.

Finally, privacy awareness should be reinforced through regular discussion. Short scenario-based exercises in team meetings—such as evaluating whether AI can safely analyze customer support tickets—help build practical judgment over time.

When embedded into everyday habits, privacy stops being a limitation and becomes a core enabler of safe, scalable AI adoption.

7.3 Clear Policies for Responsible AI Use

Your team needs guidelines. Without clear policies, people will make inconsistent decisions about when and how to use AI, causing risk, confusion, and potential harm.

Effective AI policies should not feel like restrictive rulebooks. Instead, they should act as practical frameworks that help people make good decisions quickly and confidently.

7.3.1 What an AI Policy Should Cover

A strong AI policy typically clarifies four key areas: what AI can be used for, how data should be handled, when transparency is required, and where human oversight is non-negotiable.

Acceptable and Unacceptable Uses

Start by clearly defining where AI is appropriate and where it is not. AI can be used for routine communications, summarizing documents, brainstorming, analyzing non-sensitive data, and automating low-risk tasks.

It should require approval when handling customer or employee data, making decisions that affect people, creating external communications, or deploying customer-facing tools.

It should also be explicitly prohibited from uses such as sharing confidential data with unapproved tools, making final employment-related decisions without human review, generating misleading content, or bypassing security and compliance requirements.

Data Classification and Handling

Simplify how employees assess data risk using a three-tier model:

- **Green (safe):** Public or non-sensitive information that can be freely used with AI tools
- **Yellow (caution):** Internal information that requires approved enterprise tools
- **Red (restricted):** Confidential, proprietary, or regulated data that requires strict controls and approval

This framework helps employees make quick, consistent decisions without needing technical expertise.

Transparency Requirements

Define when AI use must be disclosed. Disclosure is required when communicating with external stakeholders, publishing formal content, or making decisions that significantly affect people.

Internal brainstorming and early drafts typically do not require disclosure.

Human Oversight Requirements

Specify where human judgment must remain central. Human review is mandatory for employment-related decisions, sensitive customer communications, legal or financial outputs, and any situation where errors could cause significant harm.

In these areas, AI should support decision-making rather than replace it. For lower-risk tasks such as routine automation or internal drafting, AI can be used with lighter oversight.

> **Bonus Online Resources**
>
> Access the online resources for a customizable Responsible AI Use Policy template that can be adapted for your organization.

7.3.2 Implementing Your Policy Effectively

A policy only works if people understand and use it. Simply publishing it is not enough—you need to actively teach it and reinforce it in daily work.

Start by running a short, practical session. Walk through real scenarios, not abstract rules. For example:

- "You want to summarize a customer contract. Is this allowed?"
  (It depends on the tool being used and the type of contract.)
- "You're drafting a job posting with AI. What do you need to do?"

  (Use an approved tool, check for bias, and disclose if it's externally facing.)

Make the policy easy to access. Store it in a shared location such as a team wiki, Slack channel, or internal drive, and include a simple one-page summary for quick reference.

Keep it updated. AI tools and use cases evolve quickly, so the policy should evolve as well. On a quarterly basis, review:

- What questions are coming up that the policy doesn't address?

- Have new tools been introduced that require guidance?
- Have any incidents or mistakes revealed gaps in the policy?

Lead by example. If you violate your own policy, your team will ignore it. Model the behavior you expect: disclose when you use AI, ask for approval when needed, and admit when you're unsure.

Manager's Moment

A risk management manager was tasked with rolling out her organization's first AI policy, governing how employees could safely use emerging tools while protecting data, clients, and the company's reputation. Her past policy launches had struggled: documents were posted, emails were sent, and compliance lagged. This time, she took a different approach. Instead of starting with rules, she started with real situations employees were already facing, such as using AI to draft emails, summarize reports, or analyze data. She built the policy around those use cases, clearly outlining what was allowed, what required caution, and what was off-limits. Rather than a dense document, she created short, role-specific guides and quick-reference scenarios that answered the question employees were actually asking: *"What does this mean for my day-to-day work?"*

To ensure the policy was not just read but adopted, she shifted from announcement to engagement. She hosted brief, interactive sessions where teams walked through realistic examples, discussed gray areas, and even tested prompts together. Managers were equipped to reinforce expectations in team meetings, and early adopters were invited to share how they were using AI responsibly. She also created a simple feedback loop, allowing employees

> to ask questions, flag unclear situations, and suggest improvements. Over time, the policy evolved from a static rulebook into a shared framework for decision-making. Compliance improved as understanding deepened, and employees could see how the policy helped them use AI with confidence rather than uncertainty.

Try This Week

Conduct a bias audit:

Pick one process where you're using or considering using AI (hiring, performance reviews, customer interactions, etc.). Analyze the last 90 days of outcomes. Are there any patterns that suggest differential treatment of different groups? If you don't have enough data yet, set up tracking now so you can audit in the future.

Alternative: Review your current AI tools against the privacy checklist in this chapter. For each tool, answer: Where does our data go? Who has access? Is it used for training? If you can't answer these questions confidently, schedule time to research or contact vendors.

When You're Ready

Draft your team's AI policy:

Use the sample framework in this chapter as a starting point. Customize it for your team's specific context, tools, and risks. Share a draft with 2-3 team members and get feedback. Don't aim for perfection—aim for clarity and practicality.

Schedule a quarterly AI ethics review:

Block 60 minutes every quarter to review:

- AI tool usage and outcomes
- Any bias concerns or privacy incidents
- Policy updates needed
- Team feedback on what's working and what's not

Make ethics and trust a standing agenda item, not a one-time initiative.

PART 4

Building Your AI-Ready Plan

You understand AI. You've used it personally. You know how to roll it out and how to set ethical guardrails. Now it's time to move from understanding to execution—turning everything so far into a concrete plan you can start applying immediately and sustain over time.

The mindset shift is subtle but important: you are no longer learning about AI; you are leading with it. The habits you build here will compound over time, shaping how you and your team adapt as technology continues to evolve.

In GPS terms, this is the 🎯 Arriving phase. The system confirms: "You have arrived." But in real navigation, arrival is never the end—it simply means you're ready to set a new destination and begin the next journey with greater clarity.

Part 4 brings everything together through:

- A 30-day turn-by-turn action plan
- A simple system for staying current as AI continues to evolve
- Practical strategies for helping others build their own capability and direction

Remember: this is not about achieving perfection in 30 days, but about building momentum through small, consistent actions and visible progress. By the end of this phase, you are no longer just exploring AI; you are confidently working with it, equipped with a roadmap that extends beyond this book.

CHAPTER 8

The 30-Day AI Action Plan

This chapter is your implementation roadmap—a day-by-day, week-by-week plan that takes you from "I should try AI sometime" to "AI is integrated into how my team works."

This isn't a rigid prescription. It's a flexible framework. Adapt it to your pace, your team, and your specific challenges. But commit to the timeline. Thirty days of focused effort will create habits that last.

Week 1: Explore and Experiment

Goal: Build personal confidence with AI tools through low-stakes experimentation.

Daily Checklist

Day 1: Choose Your First Tool

- ☐ Review the tools mentioned in Chapters 3-5
- ☐ Pick one tool that solves your biggest current pain point
- ☐ Spend 10 minutes exploring the interface

Recommended starting tools:

- ChatGPT (free) - for writing, brainstorming, summarizing
- Otter.ai (free) - for meeting notes
- Notion AI (if you use Notion) - for document work

Day 2: Apply AI to a Simple Work Task

- [ ] Identify one task you do today that AI could help with
- [ ] Use your chosen tool to complete it
- [ ] Compare: How long did it take with AI vs. your usual method?
- [ ] Note what worked and what didn't (keep a simple log)

Example: Summarize a long email thread or draft a response to a routine request.

Day 3: Experiment With Prompts

- [ ] Take yesterday's task and try it again with different prompts
- [ ] Test at least 3 different ways of asking AI for the same thing
- [ ] Save your best-performing prompt in a document

Day 4: Try a Different Use Case

- [ ] Pick a different task from a different category (if Day 2 was writing, try research or analysis today)
- [ ] Use AI for this new task
- [ ] Start building your "AI wins" list—tasks where AI genuinely helped

Day 5: Reflect and Plan

- [ ] Review your week: What did AI do well? Where did it struggle?
- [ ] Identify one specific task you'll tackle with AI next week (something real, with stakes)
- [ ] Read your company's data privacy policy (prepare for Week 2's real work)

Optional but Recommended:

- Watch one 10-15 minute tutorial about your chosen tool
- Browse examples of how others in your industry use AI (Reddit, LinkedIn, YouTube)

Expected Challenges

- **"I don't have time for this."**

  Reality check: You're spending 30-45 minutes total this week. You waste more time than that in one poorly run meeting. Make the time.
- **"The AI gave me weird/wrong outputs."**

  This is normal. AI isn't reliable at first because your prompts aren't refined yet. Keep experimenting.
- **"I feel silly talking to a chatbot."**

  Everyone feels this way initially. Push through. Within days, it feels as natural as googling something.
- **"I'm not sure what tasks to try."**

  Start here: Look at your calendar and email from today. What took longer than it should have? That's your AI experiment tomorrow.

Success Indicators

By end of Week 1, you should be able to say YES to at least 3 of these:

✓ I used an AI tool on at least 4 different days

✓ I found at least 2 tasks where AI genuinely saved me time

✓ I'm starting to understand how to write better prompts

✓ I have a concrete task planned for Week 2

✓ I feel less intimidated by AI than I did on Day 1

Arriving

If you can't check 3 boxes: You're moving too fast or being too ambitious. Instead, simplify and pick easier tasks. Use AI for literally anything—even writing your grocery list—just to build the habit.

Manager's Moment

A warehouse manager for an auto parts distributor decided to try Claude to help with inventory planning and process improvements, but the experience quickly turned frustrating. He would type short, vague requests like "optimize my inventory" or "improve picking efficiency," and the responses came back generic and disconnected from the realities of his warehouse: bin locations, seasonal demand swings, supplier delays, and staffing constraints. After a few attempts, he felt like the tool wasn't built for someone like him. At that moment, he realized the problem wasn't the tool. He stopped giving vague requests and started giving clear, detailed instructions.

He provided more context: "I manage a warehouse with 12,000 SKUs, frequent backorders on brake components, and a two-shift picking operation." He defined the task: "Suggest ways to reduce picking errors and speed up fulfillment." And he specified the format: "Give me 5 practical ideas I can test this week." As a result, he received more relevant, concrete, and usable responses. He also began refining prompts, asking follow-up questions like, "Which of these would have the fastest impact?" or "How would this work with limited staff?" Over time, his confidence grew. By learning to be specific about context, task, and output, he turned an unhelpful tool into a practical assistant that could actually support his day-to-day decisions.

Week 2: Test With One Real Task

Goal: Apply AI to actual work that matters, with real stakes and real outcomes.

Weekly Checklist

Day 8: Choose Your Real Task

- ☐ Pick one important task you're doing this week (not a practice exercise—something that actually matters)
- ☐ Map out how you'd normally do it (e.g. steps, time required)
- ☐ Identify which parts AI could handle vs. which require your expertise

Tasks examples for Week 2:

- Write a project status report for stakeholders
- Prepare for a difficult conversation with a team member
- Analyze data to make a budget decision
- Draft a proposal or one-pager for leadership
- Create content for an external audience

Avoid these (too complex for Week 2):

- Anything with major legal, financial, or compliance risk
- Decisions affecting someone's employment
- Customer-facing work unless you have strong review process

Day 9-10: Execute With AI

- ☐ Use AI to complete your chosen task
- ☐ Don't just accept the first output—iterate and refine
- ☐ Track time: How long with AI vs. your estimate without AI?
- ☐ Save your prompts and the AI outputs (you'll reference these later)

Day 11: Evaluate the Outcome

- ☐ Did the work meet your quality standards? (Be honest)
- ☐ Did AI actually save time, or did wrestling with prompts take longer?
- ☐ What would you do differently next time?
- ☐ If the work is going to stakeholders, get feedback: Did they notice anything different?

Day 12: Document Your Process

- ☐ Write down exactly how you used AI for this task (step-by-step)
- ☐ Note what worked and what didn't
- ☐ Create a "recipe" you could share with someone else tackling similar work
- ☐ Decide: Is this a task you'll continue using AI for?

Expected Challenges

- **"The AI output wasn't quite right, so I had to redo everything."**
  This is the learning curve. Your first attempts will require heavy editing. By your third or fourth task, you'll know how to prompt for better initial outputs.
- **"I spent more time explaining what I wanted to AI than just doing it myself."**
  Your prompts probably need work (this improves fast with practice). Additionally, some tasks genuinely aren't good AI fits yet (that's valuable to learn)
- **"I'm nervous about the quality since this is real work."**
  Good. That nervousness keeps you vigilant. Use AI, then review like you're reviewing a junior colleague's work. Your judgment is the safety net.
- **"My task didn't go as planned—does that mean AI doesn't work?"**

No. One task isn't a valid sample size. Some tasks will click immediately while others won't. You're learning *which is which* and that's the point.

Success Indicators

By end of Week 2, you should be able to say YES to at least 3 of these:

✓ I used AI for a task that actually mattered to my work

✓ The final output met or exceeded my quality standards

✓ I can articulate what AI did well and where it struggled

✓ I saved measurable time (even if just 20-30 minutes)

✓ I have a documented process I could repeat or teach someone

If you're struggling: Pick an easier task. Week 2 isn't about proving AI is magic. It's about one successful, meaningful use case that builds your confidence.

Manager's Moment

A real estate manager began experimenting with Perplexity AI to speed up her market research, but her early attempts felt clunky and disappointing. She would ask broad questions like "What's happening in the housing market?" and get answers that are technically correct but too generic to guide real decisions. It felt like scrolling through another set of articles, only faster. After a few tries, she questioned whether the tool was actually useful for her day-to-day work of pricing homes, advising clients, and tracking local trends.

Instead of giving up, she refined her approach. She started asking more targeted questions: "What are current pricing trends for 3-bedroom homes in [specific city] over the past 90 days?" or "What factors are driving inventory changes in my market this quarter?" She also began using follow-up prompts to dig deeper and compare sources. The responses became sharper, more relevant, and easier to act on. Over time, she grew more comfortable as she learned how to work with it more effectively. What once felt like a frustrating experiment became a reliable way to quickly gather insights, validate assumptions, and enter client conversations better prepared.

Week 3: Share Successes and Challenges

Goal: Bring your team into the conversation. Share what you've learned, gather input, and identify early adopters.

Weekly Checklist

Day 15: Prepare Your Findings

- ☐ Create a simple 1-2 page summary of your AI experiments:
    - What you tried
    - What worked (with specific time/quality metrics)
    - What didn't work
    - What you learned
- ☐ Include screenshots or examples
- ☐ Be honest about failures as credibility matters more than hype

Day 16: Share With Your Team

- ☐ Schedule a 15-20 minute team meeting (or add to existing meeting)
- ☐ Present your findings (use the script from Chapter 6 if helpful)

- [ ] Emphasize: "This is optional. I'm sharing because I found it useful. Curious if others want to try?"
- [ ] Invite questions and concerns

Day 17: One-on-One Conversations

- [ ] Reach out individually to 2-3 team members who showed interest
- [ ] Offer to help them identify a task AI could help with
- [ ] Provide your documented process from Week 2 as a template
- [ ] Offer support if they're interested

Day 18: Create a Shared Resource

- [ ] Set up a simple shared space (Slack channel, shared doc, wiki page) for AI learnings
- [ ] Post your Week 2 process as the first entry
- [ ] Invite teams to share their own experiments (when they're ready)
- [ ] Establish norm: "Share wins *and* failures as both are valuable"

Day 19: Identify Your Champions

- [ ] Note who expressed genuine interest (not just politeness)
- [ ] Reach out: "I noticed you seemed interested in [AI use case]. Want to pilot this together next week?"
- [ ] Aim for 2-3 champions (if you get even 1, that's success)

Reflection:

- How did your team react? Excited? Skeptical? Indifferent?
- Adjust your Week 4 plan based on their readiness level

Expected Challenges

- **"Most of my team seemed uninterested or skeptical."**
  This is normal. Not everyone will be an early adopter. Focus on the 15-20% who are curious. They'll influence the others later through peer effect.
- **"Someone asked a question I couldn't answer about data privacy/security."**
  Perfect opportunity. Answer honestly: "Great question. I don't know the answer. Let me find out and get back to you." Then actually find out (review Chapter 7 or contact your IT/security team).
- **"People were worried about job security."**
  Address directly. Use the communication strategies from Chapter 6: "AI handles tasks, not jobs.
  The tedious stuff we all dislike. Your judgment, relationships, creativity—those are irreplaceable."
- **"I got pushback: 'We don't have time to learn new tools.'"**
  Empathize, then reframe. "I hear you. That's why I'm not asking you to learn anything yet. I'm sharing what saved me [X hours] this week. If that sounds useful for the kind of work you do, I'm happy to help. If not, no worries."

Success Indicators

By end of Week 3, you should have:

✓ Shared your AI experience with your team (even if response was mixed)

✓ Had meaningful conversations with at least 2 team members about AI

✓ Identified 1-3 potential champions willing to experiment

✓ Created a space for ongoing AI learning and sharing

✓ Addressed at least one concern or objection with honesty

If nobody's interested: Don't force it as some teams need more time. Continue using AI yourself, share occasional wins organically, and revisit formal introduction in 4-6 weeks. Some teams need to see sustained value before they're ready to try.

Manager's Moment

A school principal saw strong potential in using Gemini to support lesson planning, differentiation, and administrative workload, but his teachers were unconvinced. Their experience with AI had been negative: catching students submitting AI-generated essays that were often shallow, inaccurate, or disconnected from classroom expectations. To them, AI felt more like a shortcut to avoid learning than a tool to enhance it. Early attempts to introduce Gemini through emails and optional training fell flat. The teachers didn't need another tool, they needed a reason to trust it.

So the principal changed his approach. Instead of promoting AI in general, he focused on teacher-specific use cases. In a staff meeting, he demonstrated how Gemini could take a standard lesson and generate three differentiated versions for varying reading levels, a process that normally took hours. He invited teachers to bring real materials and experiment in small groups, comparing outputs and refining prompts together. Acknowledging the limitations they had seen, he presented AI as support for teacher preparation, rather than a replacement for student thinking. Gradually, skepticism softened. Teachers began using it to draft rubrics, generate discussion questions, and brainstorm activities,

> always reviewing and adapting the results. They developed a clearer understanding of how to use the tool effectively.

Week 4: Roll Out to Wider Scope

Goal: Scale from individual experimentation to team adoption with sustainable practices.

Weekly Checklist

Day 22: Launch a Pilot Program

- ☐ Based on Week 3 conversations, choose one specific use case for team pilot
- ☐ Work with your champions to define:
    - What task we're piloting (be specific)
    - Who's participating (volunteers only)
    - How long we'll pilot (suggest 2 weeks)
    - What success looks like (measurable)
- ☐ Send invitation to other team members (optional participation)

Example pilot programs:

- "For the next 2 weeks, volunteers will use Otter.ai in team meetings. We'll evaluate time savings and accuracy."
- "Marketing team will use ChatGPT to draft social media posts (with human review). We'll compare output volume and quality."
- "Support team will test AI email templates for common customer questions. We'll track response time and satisfaction."

Day 23: Set Up Infrastructure

- ☐ Ensure everyone has access to the needed tools (accounts, licenses, etc.)
- ☐ Share the AI policy you drafted in Chapter 7 (or create simple guidelines)
- ☐ Create a quick-reference guide: "How to use [Tool] for [Task] in 5 steps"
- ☐ Establish check-in rhythm (suggest mid-pilot and end-of-pilot reviews)

Day 24: Provide Support

- ☐ Host 15-minute "office hours" where people can ask questions
- ☐ Check in with champions: "How's it going? Any blockers?"
- ☐ Address any technical issues or confusion quickly
- ☐ Share early wins in team channel (with permission): "Sarah used AI to summarize client feedback—saved 90 minutes!"

Day 25: Monitor and Adjust

- ☐ Review pilot progress at midpoint
- ☐ Ask participants:
    - What's working?
    - What's frustrating?
    - What would make this more useful?
- ☐ Make quick adjustments if needed (better prompts, different workflows, etc.)
- ☐ Recognize participants publicly (they're taking a risk to help the team learn)

Day 26: Plan for Sustainability

- [ ] Based on pilot progress, start planning what happens after the 30 days:
    - Which AI use cases should continue?
    - Who will support ongoing adoption (you can't be a single point of contact forever)?
    - What training or resources does the team need?
    - How will we handle new team members?
- [ ] Draft a simple "What's Next" plan for Week 5 and beyond

Reflection:

- [ ] Review your full 30-day journey: What changed from Day 1 to Day 30?
- [ ] Celebrate progress (even if it's smaller than you hoped)
- [ ] Identify 1-2 specific commitments for continued AI leadership

Expected Challenges

- **"The pilot isn't going as smoothly as I hoped."**

  Perfect. Pilots exist to surface problems in controlled environments. Document what's not working and why.

- **"Some people are using AI, but not following the guidelines."**

  Address directly but kindly. Pull them aside: "I noticed you're using AI for [task]. That's great! Quick question: are you familiar with our policy on [data privacy/review requirements/etc.]? Let's make sure we're aligned."

- **"I'm spending too much time supporting everyone's questions."**

  This is why you identified champions. Empower them: "You've got this down. When [teammate] has questions, can you help them? I'll back you up if you get stuck."

- **"Results are mixed—some people love it, others see no value."**

  This is success, not failure. Some roles/tasks benefit more than others. Focus on expanding where it works, not forcing it where it doesn't.

- **"My boss is asking why we're spending time on this."**

  Come prepared with data. "We've saved [X hours] across the team in the pilot. That's [Y hours/year] if we continue. Additionally, we've identified [Z specific improvements] in quality/speed/decision-making. The ROI is clear."

Success Indicators

By end of Week 4 (Day 30), you should have:

✓ At least 3-5 team members actively using AI for specific tasks

✓ Documented time savings or quality improvements from pilot

✓ A sustainable plan for ongoing AI adoption (not dependent on you alone)

✓ Clear understanding of which use cases work well for your team

✓ Reduced your own time on routine tasks by at least 10-20%

✓ Team members who are now champions (voluntarily helping others)

More important than any checklist: You've shifted from "I should learn about AI" to "AI is part of how my team works." That mindset shift is the real victory.

Manager's Moment

A manager overseeing a team of forest rangers was eager to introduce Claude to improve reporting, incident documentation, and planning, but her team resisted. Most of the rangers didn't see themselves as "computer people." They had chosen the job because they loved being outside, not behind a screen, and anything that felt like more desk work was met with quiet resistance. Early attempts to train them on AI features fell flat. The turning point came when the manager redefined the tool as something that brought them closer to the field.

She started by demonstrating a simple, tangible use case: after a long day, a ranger could dictate rough notes about trail conditions, wildlife sightings, or visitor incidents, and Claude could turn it into a clean, complete report in seconds. She also showed how the tool could summarize long policy updates into quick bullet points and help draft permit responses without starting from scratch. Instead of formal training, she held short, informal sessions where rangers tried it on their own real tasks. As they saw that AI reduced paperwork rather than added to it, interest grew. Over time, the tool became less of a burden and more of a shortcut, quietly handling the administrative work so they could spend more time where they actually wanted to be: out in the forest.

What Happens on Day 31?

Here's your bonus Week 5 playbook:

- **Continue personally using AI daily.** Even just one task. The skill atrophies if you stop practicing.
- **Hold monthly AI learning sessions.** Set 30 minutes aside, where someone shares a new use case and the team discusses. This approach keeps learning alive.
- **Track metrics quarterly.** How much time are we saving? What new capabilities have we unlocked? What's the ROI?
- **Revisit your policy.** As you learn, update guidelines. Add new approved tools. Adjust based on what's working.
- **Celebrate wins publicly.** When someone has an AI success, share it. Recognition drives adoption.
- **Stay curious.** New tools and capabilities emerge constantly. Dedicate 15 minutes/week to staying current.

The 30-day plan gets you started. The habits you build determine whether AI becomes a lasting competitive advantage or a forgotten experiment.

Try This Week

Actually start Day 1 of the plan. Not "eventually." Not "when things calm down." Block 30 minutes on your calendar. Pick your tool. Do your first experiment.

The difference between managers who successfully adopt AI and those who don't isn't knowledge. It's action. You have the knowledge. Take the first step.

When You're Ready

Customize this plan for your team. The framework is solid, but your team is unique. Adjust timelines, tasks, and success metrics to fit your reality. Then commit to the adjusted version.

Find an accountability partner. Say another manager in your organization is also interested in AI. Share your 30-day plans. Check in weekly. You're 3x more likely to complete the plan if someone's checking in on your progress.

CHAPTER 9

Future-Proofing Your Skills

You've completed your 30-day plan. You're using AI and your team is experimenting with it too. Now comes the next challenge: How do you stay current as AI evolves without burning out, without feeling like you're constantly falling behind, without becoming enslaved to tech news?

This chapter gives you sustainable strategies for continuous learning. The goal is simple: Build habits that let you adapt confidently to whatever comes next, whether that's new AI capabilities, new tools, or entirely new ways of working.

9.1 How to Keep Learning Without Being Glued to Tech News

The AI landscape changes constantly—new models launch, existing tools add features, and headlines swing between breakthroughs and warnings. Trying to keep up with everything can quickly become exhausting.

Many managers assume staying current requires hours of reading and nonstop attention. In reality, it requires something much simpler: consistency and curation.

Let's look at how to build a learning habit that keeps you informed without pulling you into the endless cycle of tech news.

9.1.1 The 15-Minute Weekly Learning Habit

Every Monday (or Friday—pick what works), spend 15 minutes doing this:

Minutes 1-7: Scan curated sources

Don't browse random AI news. Follow 2-3 high-quality, low-noise sources that filter signals from hype.

Recommended sources (pick 2):

- **The Rundown AI** (newsletter) - Daily 5-minute AI news summary; focus on practical business applications
- **TLDR AI** (newsletter) - Tech-focused but accessible; highlights what matters for non-engineers
- **Matt Wolfe's YouTube channel** - Weekly roundups of new AI tools; shows them in action
- **Ben's Bites** (newsletter) - Fast-paced AI news; good for staying aware of major developments

What you're looking for:

- New capabilities in tools you already use
- Emerging use cases relevant to your industry
- Major shifts (regulatory changes, new model releases, security issues)

Minutes 8-12: Ask yourself two questions

1. **"Is there anything here I should try this week?"**
    - New feature in a tool I use?
    - Use case I hadn't considered?
    - Something addressing a current team pain point?
2. **"Is there anything here I need to discuss with my team?"**
    - Security/privacy concerns affecting our tools?

- Capability that changes what's possible for us?
- Industry shift we should be aware of?

Minutes 13-15: Take one action

Don't just consume—act. Pick the smallest possible next step:

- Bookmark one article to read later
- Try one new feature
- Share one insight with team
- Add one item to your AI backlog

The power of this habit: 15 minutes × 52 weeks = 13 hours/year of focused learning. That's enough to stay current without drowning in information.

9.1.2 The "Just-in-Time Learning" Approach

Instead of learning everything proactively, learn what you need when you need it. When you encounter a new problem or opportunity, that's when you invest time learning.

Example

Your team starts working with international clients. Now you spend 30 minutes learning about AI translation tools. Not before, when it was theoretical.

OR

You need to analyze customer feedback at scale. *Now* you learn about AI sentiment analysis tools. Not six months ago when you had no use for it.

This approach prevents two traps:

1. Learning things you'll never use (wasted time)
2. Forgetting things before you need them (wasted learning)

9.1.3 Build a Learning Backlog, Not a Reading List

Most managers have dozens of saved articles they'll never read which is demotivating. Instead, keep a simple "AI Learning Backlog" with three columns:

Table 9.1 Sample AI Learning Backlog

Now (This Month)	Next (Next 2-3 Months)	Someday (Parking Lot)
• 2-3 things you're actively learning or implementing	• 3-5 things you want to explore when current priorities are done	• Everything else that seems interesting but isn't urgent
• Example: "Master ChatGPT advanced prompting" or "Implement AI meeting notes for team"	• Example: "Investigate AI for budget forecasting" or "Learn about AI coding assistants"	• Review quarterly; most items will become irrelevant and can be deleted

You're not trying to learn everything. You're intentionally choosing what matters most right now.

9.1.4 The "Teach to Learn" Method

The fastest way to solidify your AI knowledge is to teach it to someone else. Once a month, share one thing you learned:

- Host a 10-minute team demo of a new AI feature
- Write a quick Slack post about a use case you discovered
- Help a colleague implement something you've already figured out

Teaching and explaining concepts reveals gaps in your own knowledge, which you can then work to fill, while helping others reinforces your skills through repeated practice.

Manager's Moment

A hotel manager at a busy downtown property wanted to stay current on AI without drowning in hype. Every week seemed to bring a flood of new tools, bold claims, and conflicting advice. Instead of chasing everything, he built a simple rhythm: he used Perplexity AI to scan for credible updates in hospitality and operations, focusing on sources with real-world examples. He asked questions like, *"What new AI tools are hotels using to improve guest check-in or housekeeping efficiency?"* and *"Which of these have proven ROI?"* This helped him filter out buzzwords and focus on what was actually being used in hotels similar to his. He kept a short list of ideas, but only a few made it past his first filter: relevance, simplicity, and immediate applicability.

When sharing with his team, he focused on bringing one practical idea at a time into team meetings such as using AI to draft personalized guest responses or summarize guest feedback into themes. He explained it in plain terms, showed a quick example, and invited staff to try it on a real task. By using a trial-and-error approach, he built trust with his team. They didn't feel pressured to keep up with everything because they trusted him to focus on what mattered. As a result, his staff developed their interests and skills in using AI. Before long, they began sharing practical ideas for its use.

Over time, you also build a reputation as a trusted AI resource within your organization—an advantage that can strengthen both your visibility and career growth.

9.2 Networking With AI-Savvy Leaders

You cannot navigate AI adoption in isolation. The managers who progress fastest are usually the ones learning from peers who are further ahead while also sharing insights with those who are just getting started.

9.2.1 Find Your AI Peer Group

Within Your Organization

Identify 2-3 other managers who are also experimenting with AI. Create an informal peer learning group.

How it works:

- Meet monthly (30-45 minutes, virtual is fine)
- Rotating format: Each person shares one AI win and one AI struggle
- Help each other troubleshoot
- Share prompts, workflows, tool recommendations

Peers understand your company's culture, data policies, and specific constraints. Their solutions are more directly applicable than generic advice.

Beyond Your Organization

Join one external community where AI-savvy managers gather.

Options:

- **LinkedIn groups:** Search "AI for [your industry]" - many active communities
- **Slack/Discord communities:**
  - AI for Work (Slack community focused on practical business AI)

    - Various industry-specific AI communities

- **Local meetups:** Search Meetup.com or Eventbrite for "AI for business" in your city
- **Online cohorts:** Programs like Section 4, Reforge, or Maven run AI-focused courses with built-in peer groups

Pick one community. Don't join five and participate in none.

9.2.2 Share Your Own Journey Publicly

Once you begin seeing meaningful AI wins, share them—not to brag, but to help others learn and to strengthen your professional network.

You can share through:

- A LinkedIn post: "Here's how we used AI to reduce meeting prep time by 40%"
- Industry forums: answering questions about practical AI adoption
- Conference talks: proposing sessions on real-world AI use cases, even at smaller events
- Blog posts: documenting your 30-day journey and lessons learned

Sharing creates benefits beyond visibility. People begin reaching out with questions, which naturally expands your network. You become recognized as someone who understands practical AI adoption, strengthening your professional reputation and opening doors to conversations and opportunities you might not otherwise access.

Manager's Moment

A director at a renewable energy organization recognized that staying current with AI required more than reading articles—it meant learning alongside peers facing similar challenges. Instead of trying to track every new development alone, she began connecting with like-minded managers through industry forums, LinkedIn groups, and clean energy conferences. She followed conversations where leaders discussed how AI was being used for grid optimization, predictive maintenance, and energy demand forecasting. Tools like Claude helped her separate credible use cases from hype. Over time, she built an informal network of peers who shared what they were testing, what was working, and where they were running into obstacles.

Rather than keeping those insights to herself, she turned them into practical takeaways for her team. After each conference or discussion thread, she refined a few relevant ideas—such as improving equipment monitoring or streamline reporting with AI, and shared them in short, focused updates. She also invited team members to join select webinars or forums, gradually expanding the organization's exposure to these conversations. By learning from like-minded managers , she applied her knowledge in practice. And by curating and sharing selectively, she helped her team engage with AI that felt relevant to their work.

Bonus Online Resources

Access the online resources for a curated AI learning toolkit designed for ongoing, practical skill development. It includes selected newsletters, videos, podcasts, courses, communities, and tool directories to help managers stay updated.

9.3 Building Your Personal AI Learning System

Here's how to combine these resources into a sustainable system:

Daily (5 minutes)

- Scan one newsletter over morning coffee
- Note anything immediately relevant

Weekly (15 minutes)

- Review the week's flagged items
- Try one new thing OR go deeper on one topic
- Share one learning with your team

Monthly (30-45 minutes)

- Attend or watch one webinar/video on emerging trends
- Participate in one community discussion
- Review and update your learning backlog

Quarterly (1-2 hours)

- Take stock: What's changed in the AI landscape?
- Audit your tools: Still using them? Need replacements?
- Adjust your learning plan for next quarter
- Coffee chat with one AI-savvy peer

Annual (Half day)

- Reflect on your AI journey over the past year
- Set 2-3 goals for next year's AI capabilities
- Consider: Should you deepen expertise, expand to new areas, or focus on team enablement?

AI will continue evolving. Tools will come and go. Capabilities will expand in ways we can't imagine today.

But if you build these habits—consistent learning, peer networking, practical experimentation—you'll be ready. Not because you know everything that's coming, but because you know how to learn quickly when it does. That's what future-proofing actually means.

Manager's Moment

A manager overseeing a team of air traffic controllers realized that staying current on AI required occasional reading and a consistent, intentional learning rhythm. With limited time and a high-stakes role, she curated a small set of trusted inputs rather than trying to follow everything. She subscribed to a handful of aviation and AI newsletters focused on operational use cases, listened to short podcasts during her commute about real-world applications, and watched videos that demonstrated how AI was being used in complex systems like logistics and transportation. She went deeper by enrolling in targeted online courses on concepts like predictive analytics and anomaly detection.

She also sought out communities where practitioners were discussing what was actually working. Through industry forums, webinars, and small peer groups, she listened more than she spoke, and learned through experience. Over time, she developed a filter: if a new idea didn't connect to real operational challenges, she set it aside. If it did, she explored it further. This steady, layered approach helped her move from feeling overwhelmed by AI to developing a working fluency. She didn't try to master everything; she focused on understanding enough to ask better questions, recognize meaningful developments, and stay grounded in what truly mattered for her field.

As you close this book, remember that AI is not replacing leadership—it is becoming part of it. Like email, spreadsheets, and project management software before it, AI is quickly becoming a fundamental tool for getting work done. The managers who learn to use it thoughtfully today will gain an advantage that compounds over time, enabling them to make better decisions, communicate more effectively, and focus their energy where it matters most.

The future belongs not to managers who know the most about AI, but to those who remain curious, adaptable, and willing to learn. Use AI to enhance your capabilities, not replace your judgment. Lead with integrity, bring your team along on the journey, and continue experimenting, learning, and growing. The tools will evolve, but the need for strong, thoughtful leadership will remain—and that is where your greatest value will always lie.

Try This Week

Pick one newsletter from this chapter and subscribe. Block 15 minutes on your calendar next Monday (recurring weekly) for your AI learning habit. Just those two actions. Don't try to implement everything—start with the minimum viable learning system.

When You're Ready

Find your peer group: Identify 2-3 colleagues who are also interested in AI. Send them a message: "Want to start a monthly AI learning group? 30 minutes, share what's working and what's not?" If internal peers aren't available, join one external community from the list in this chapter.

Schedule your first coffee chat: Think of one person in your network who's ahead of you on AI adoption. Reach out this week with a specific request for a 20-minute conversation.

Further Reading

Agrawal, A., Gans, J., & Goldfarb, A. (2018). Prediction machines: The simple economics of artificial intelligence. Harvard Business Review Press.

Chandrakant, K. (2026). Artificial intelligence essentials you always wanted to know. Vibrant Publishers.

Daugherty, P. R., & Wilson, H. J. (2018). Human + machine: Reimagining work in the age of AI. Harvard Business Review Press.

Iansiti, M., & Lakhani, K. R. (2020). Competing in the age of AI: Strategy and leadership when algorithms and networks run the world. Harvard Business Review Press.

Mollick, E. (2024). Co-intelligence: Living and working with AI. Portfolio.

Suleyman, M. (2023). The coming wave: Technology, power, and the twenty-first century's greatest dilemma. Crown.

Glossary

AI (Artificial Intelligence): Technology designed to perform tasks that typically require human intelligence, such as analyzing information, recognizing patterns, generating content, or making predictions.

AI Assistant: A software tool that interacts conversationally with users to help complete tasks such as writing, summarizing, researching, analyzing data, or brainstorming ideas.

AI Policy: Organizational guidelines that define how AI tools may and may not be used, including rules related to privacy, security, ethics, and compliance.

AI-Ready: A mindset and level of preparedness in which a manager or organization can thoughtfully evaluate, adopt, and use AI tools effectively and responsibly.

Algorithm: A set of rules or instructions a computer system follows to process information or solve problems.

Analytics: The process of examining data to identify patterns, trends, insights, or opportunities for improvement.

Anomaly Detection: The identification of unusual patterns or behaviors in data that may indicate errors, risks, fraud, or emerging issues.

API (Application Programming Interface): A mechanism that allows different software systems to communicate and exchange information with each other.

Automation: The use of technology to complete repetitive or routine tasks with minimal human intervention.

Bias (AI Bias): Systematic unfairness in AI outputs or decisions caused by flawed data, assumptions, or algorithms.

Business Intelligence (BI): Technologies and processes used to analyze organizational data and support better business decision-making.

Change Adoption: The process by which individuals and teams begin accepting, using, and integrating new systems, tools, or ways of working.

Chatbot: A conversational software program that interacts with users through text or voice.

Claude: An AI assistant developed by Anthropic known for handling long documents, analysis, and writing tasks.

CRM (Customer Relationship Management): A system used to manage relationships, communication, and data related to customers, donors, or clients.

Data Privacy: The protection of sensitive or personal information from unauthorized access, sharing, or misuse.

Data Visualization: The presentation of information through charts, graphs, dashboards, or other visual formats to make insights easier to understand.

Deep Learning: A branch of machine learning that uses layered neural networks to identify patterns and make predictions from large amounts of data.

DeepL Pro: An AI-powered translation platform designed for high-quality written language translation.

Digital Transformation: The integration of digital technologies into organizational processes, workflows, and services.

ERP (Enterprise Resource Planning): Software used to manage core organizational functions such as finance, procurement, inventory, and operations.

ERM (Enterprise Risk Management): A structured approach for identifying, assessing, and managing organizational risks across the enterprise.

Ethical AI: The responsible development and use of AI systems in ways that are fair, transparent, safe, and aligned with human values.

Forecasting: The use of historical data, trends, and assumptions to predict future outcomes or performance.

Generative AI: AI systems capable of creating original content such as text, images, audio, code, or summaries.

Gemini: An AI assistant developed by Google and integrated into many Google products and services.

Hallucination (AI Hallucination): An incorrect or fabricated AI response presented confidently as factual information.

Human-in-the-Loop: A process where humans review, guide, or validate AI outputs before final decisions are made.

Knowledge Management: The process of organizing, storing, sharing, and maintaining organizational knowledge and information.

Large Language Model (LLM): A type of AI model trained on massive amounts of text data to understand and generate human-like language.

Machine Learning: A branch of AI in which systems learn patterns from data to improve performance over time without explicit programming for every task.

Natural Language Processing (NLP): Technology that enables computers to understand, interpret, and generate human language.

Notion AI: An AI assistant integrated into the Notion productivity platform to assist with writing, organization, and workflow tasks.

Perplexity AI: An AI-powered research and search assistant designed to provide summarized answers with cited sources.

Power BI: A business analytics and visualization platform developed by Microsoft.

Predictive Analytics: The use of data, statistical models, and AI to forecast future outcomes or behaviors.

Prompt: The instruction, question, or request given to an AI system.

Prompt Engineering: The practice of crafting effective prompts that improve the quality, relevance, and accuracy of AI responses.

Retrieval-Augmented Generation (RAG): An AI approach that combines language generation with access to external documents or databases for more accurate answers.

Scenario Planning: A strategic method of exploring possible future situations and their potential impact on decisions or operations.

Sentiment Analysis: AI analysis used to identify emotional tone or attitudes within text or conversations.

Sprint Planning: An Agile project management activity where teams define work and priorities for a short development cycle called a sprint.

Structured Prompt: A prompt that includes clear context, task instructions, constraints, and desired output format.

Token: A unit of text processed by AI systems. Tokens may represent words, parts of words, or characters.

Training Data: The information used to teach AI systems patterns, relationships, and language behavior.

Transparency: The degree to which AI systems and decisions can be understood, explained, or reviewed.

Workflow: The sequence of tasks, activities, or processes required to complete work.

Workday: A cloud-based enterprise platform used for human resources, payroll, workforce planning, and analytics.

Zero-Shot Prompting: Asking an AI system to perform a task without providing examples first.

Made in the USA
Monee, IL
13 September 2026

62975268R00095